Godwink

STORIES

A Devotional

Godwink

STORIES

A Devotional

SQuire Rushnell

Louise DuArt

 HOWARD BOOKS
A DIVISION OF SIMON & SCHUSTER, INC.

New York   Nashville   London   Toronto   Sydney   New Delhi

Howard Books
A Division of Simon & Schuster, Inc.
1230 Avenue of the Americas
New York, NY 10020

First Howard Books hardcover edition December 2012

HOWARD and colophon are trademarks of Simon & Schuster, Inc.

For information about special discounts for bulk purchases, please contact Simon & Schuster Special Sales at 1-866-506-1949 or business@simonandschuster.com.

The Simon & Schuster Speakers Bureau can bring authors to your live event. For more information or to book an event, contact the Simon & Schuster Speakers Bureau at 1-866-248-3049 or visit our website at www.simonspeakers.com.

Designed by Carla Jayne Jones

Manufactured in the United States of America

10   9   8   7   6   5   4   3   2

Library of Congress Cataloging-in-Publication Data
Rushnell, Squire D.
    Godwink stories: a devotional / Squire Rushnell.
        p.   cm.
    1. Christian life—Miscellanea. 2. Spiritual life—Christianity—Miscellanea. 3. Spirituality—Miscellanea. I. Title.
    BV4501.3.R867   2012
    242—dc23   2012019965

ISBN 978-1-4516-7856-7
ISBN 978-1-4516-7859-8 (ebook)

To Grace DuArt and Mafawna Rushnell,
two wonderful mothers who birthed
the birthers of this book.

—Louise and SQuire

Contents

A Personal Note to You

Dear Reader,

I want to thank you for picking up Godwink Stories. *May I point out a few things?*

The centerpiece of this book is the collection of charming, heartfelt, and astonishing letters I have received from people just like you who have taken the time to share their life-altering godwink stories.

These warm letters reaffirm that godwinks happen to everyone. We just need to learn how to see them, allow them to unfold, and accept them as direct, person-to-person communications from God to each of us.

As you'll see, every note, buoyant with enthusiasm, is from someone like a new friend of yours who tells you that those so-called coincidences you'd been dismissing really do mean something. And you need to pay attention. They are like unopened gifts that have been placed upon your doorstep.

If you're like me, you will also be impressed at how every joy, every hurt, and every worry you encounter has already been written about in the Bible. Godwink Stories *simply draws upon the parallel between the letters of real people and the wisdom God had others write into the ancient Scriptures three thousand years ago.*

Unlike my other When God Winks *books, this one is coauthored with my wonderful wife, Louise DuArt. I may be the storyteller in the family, but she is our in-house authority on the Scriptures. Therefore, anytime this book uses the pronoun* I, *you should know that it reflects the way we live our lives: three as one—God, my wife, and myself.*

Finally, Godwink Stories *can be read in various ways. You may decide to read the book cover to cover. You may wish to place it on your night table to read one bite-size mini-chapter per week for fifty-two weeks. Or you may just want a pick-me-up story that fits your need of the day.*

For the latter purpose, Godwink Stories *is cross-referenced by category—suiting your desire to peruse a letter that speaks to a time of sorrow or your appetite for an uplifting bedtime story.*

Along the way, perhaps you'll be inspired to write your own Godwink story. Can't wait to read it!

You may share your letter by writing to one of these addresses:

* squire@whengodwinks.com
* facebook.com/GODwinks
* Godwink Stories
  P.O. Box 36
  Edgartown, MA 02539

Have a wonderful read, and good wishes for abundant godwinks!

SQuire and Louise

1

How Can I Shake My Unhappiness?

Is any one of you in trouble?
He should pray.
Is anyone happy?
Let him sing songs of praise.

James 5:13 NIV

Are you happy?

Perhaps you'll say you have problems that prevent happiness such as:

- People are not treating you with respect.

- Or maybe you've been "unlucky"; born into a burdensome life.

Does that sound like you?

If so, you may ask, Why are those reasons for being unhappy justified for you, but not for others who are worse off than you? People in more lowly jobs than yours, with worse handicaps? Yet who greet each day whistling and smiling? Or how about those who are sitting in wheelchairs, unable to feed themselves, who nonetheless always have something cheerful to say and are never heard to blame their circumstances? If so, don't worry.

These people have discovered a secret, but it's a secret that belongs to you as much as it belongs to them. It's this: happiness is not something you are bequeathed at birth, like wealth or poverty; it is not something you earn through hard work, like a college education; and it is not something given to you because of your dialect or skin color.

Happiness is a state of mind that you choose for yourself.

Being happy cannot be attributed to circumstances—though many try—and cannot be dependent on someone else—though many think it is.

Happiness is something you can have, right now.

Just by choosing.

Your operator's manual—the Bible—says:

> *When times are good, be happy;*
> *but when times are bad, consider:*

2

God has made the one as well as the other.
Ecclesiastes 7:14 NIV

People who are happy have chosen to adopt an optimistic attitude and to approach every day in an intimate partnership with God.

> *This is the day the LORD has made;*
> *let us rejoice and be glad in it.*
> Psalm 118:24 NIV

So ask yourself, "Am I happy?"
If the answer is no, ask, "Do I *want* to be?"
Janet Marie Withers wrote about a friend who was known for asking people that all-important question:

Are Ya Happy?

My dear friend Sebastian died in December. We worked together and were best friends.

Sebastian always used a personal greeting with me. Whenever he'd come by my desk, he would smile and say, "Are ya happy?"

The day I found out Sebastian had passed away, I was in shock. I left work and prayed for a sign from God that some essence of Sebastian would still survive, in spirit, and that somehow my grief could be heard.

I had to mail a Christmas package. I didn't feel up to it but decided to go to the post office anyway. As I stood in line, a big man in front of me, about the size of Sebastian, turned and casually asked, "Are ya happy?"

I nearly fainted.

I thought I hadn't heard him right. Fumbling for words, I finally spilled out: "I'm overwhelmed!"

He smiled gently, turned, and moved forward in line.

I haven't heard that phrase used often, except with my dear Sebastian. It's not a typical greeting. I wanted to believe that, somehow, God and Sebastian were reaching out to me from beyond.

I left the post office with a surreal feeling—still unconvinced, still holding on to my grief and pain; still shrugging it off as just a coincidence.

Days later, my son and I were at McDonald's. An older woman chatted us up and then, suddenly, paused. She looked at me and said, "There's a book I sense you need."

She wrote the title and author's name on an envelope. I kept it until I got home. I was going to throw it away . . . not feeling like receiving any pep talks. But I kept it.

On Christmas morning I opened a gift from my sister, Dorothy, and there it was—that very book—*When God Winks at You: How God Speaks Directly to You Through the Power of Coincidence*, by SQuire Rushnell.

I excitedly showed my sister the note given to me by the woman I'd met at McDonald's.

Now it all makes sense. It's a comfort to know that hearing Sebastian's phrase, "Are ya happy," was no coincidence: it was a godwink!

Janet Marie Withers

What a wonderful lesson from Janet. It makes us wish we all could have known Sebastian. He seems like the type of person who never wandered around telling everyone what a bad day he was having, what terrible things others were doing to him, or what a difficult hand he'd been dealt since birth. Instead, Sebastian chose to be happy. It was that simple.

So can you.

Sebastian was in sync with this teaching from the ancient Scriptures:

> *I know that there is nothing better for men*
> *than to be happy and do good while they*
> *live.*

Ecclesiastes 3:12 NIV

Today, decide for yourself whether you are going to look at the glass as half full or half empty. It's your choice. Yours and God's. And He wants your glass to be overflowing.

Try being a Sebastian today. Are ya happy?

2

How Does God Help Me with My Medical Problems?

When I called, you answered me;
you made me bold and stouthearted.

Psalm 138:3 NIV

Part of the delight in authoring the *When God Winks* books is discovering where they are taking me. I distinctly remember the day the word *godwink* blossomed in my mind . . . and thinking, My, what a friendly little word. Then saying, "Thank you Lord, for placing it there." A word to fill a vacancy in the language for so-called coincidences that you are certain could not be coincidence.

It was another delight when the term *Godwink Link* popped into my head, for it seemed to perfectly identify the

6

person who is the deliverer of a godwink to you or me—the unwitting messenger who "just happens" to make a phone call at the perfect moment to provide encouragement; or bumps into you, out of the blue, and changes the course of your life through a new job or relationship; or places something precisely where you'll see it for the purpose of giving you necessary information.

In fact, we are all Godwink Links at one time or another—innocent couriers for God, brightening someone's day, or in some cases, providing that person with life-saving information.

That was the role of Dolly's friend—a Godwink Link—as Dolly describes it in her letter.

Dolly's Godwink Link

My husband and I annually visit close friends, Patty and her husband, at their cabin in West Virginia for a fun weekend. This particular visit was a godwink for me.

Patty and I were in the kitchen, and she told me she'd gone to the dermatologist for a checkup the week before. While waiting to see the doctor, she watched a video about skin cancer. It raised her concern at first, but the doctor gave her great news—she was fine.

I was at the sink doing the dishes, wearing a tank top, when she came over to me and said, "Dolly, you have a mole on your back that looks funny, you should have it looked at."

I laughed and said, "Since you saw that video, you're going to be all over us."

Well, wouldn't you know, I was divinely aligned to have a routine doctor's appointment of my own the following week. The doctor talked with me, did everything he needed to do, and I was getting up to leave when I heard an inner voice say, "The mole."

I turned to the doctor and said, "Oh yes, I have a mole on my back that my friend said I should have looked at."

He examined it. "It does look a little funny," he said casually. "Let's take a biopsy."

Three days later he telephoned and said, "Dolly, I am as shocked as you. It's melanoma."

I promptly went in for surgery, the doctor got it all, and I've felt good ever since. I asked him, "How long would you have given me if I hadn't found this when I did?"

He looked at me seriously and said, "About two years."

Isn't it wonderful the way God works? He used my friend to alert me to the mole on my back because He knew I would never see it and had no other reason to see a dermatologist.

I praise God all the time for using my friend as my Godwink Link.

Thank you for letting me share my story. I love telling it.

Dolly Estep

Isn't that just the way God works?

- Patty "just happened" to have the information Dolly needed, having seen a video.

- Dolly "just happened" to wear a tank top that day.
- Patty "just happened" to see a mole that Dolly couldn't possibly see.
- Dolly "just happened" to have a scheduled appointment with the doctor.
- The doctor was now divinely aligned to test the mole and perform the surgery before the melanoma could become a fatal problem for Dolly.

Now—tell us God had nothing to do with that!

Your heavenly Father cares for you and all His children. He knows what you need before you do. And, with loving eyes, He is always looking out for you.

If God is concerned about tiny sparrows in the sky, then how much greater is His concern for you? He considers you much more valuable than the sparrow.

> *Are not two sparrows sold for a penny?*
> *Yet not one of them will fall to the ground*
> *outside your Father's care.*
> *And even the very hairs of your head*
> *are all numbered. So don't be afraid;*
> *you are worth more than many sparrows.*
> Matthew 10:29–31 NIV

"God is watching you," say the words to a song. Another classic song tells us:

> *His eye is on the sparrow,*
> *and I know He watches me.*[1]

Yes, he does!

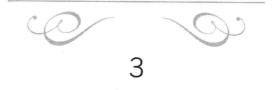

3

How Do I Discover My Purpose for God?

I am sending an angel ahead of you
to guard you along the way.

Exodus 23:20 NIV

We have a brain-injured son, Grant, who lives in one of the most exemplary communities in the world for adult disabled people. Everyone has a job. They get a paycheck. And they feel good about themselves.

Yvonne Streit, founder of Brookwood Community, says, "We show our citizens how to be proud of what they actually *can* do—especially what they *didn't think* they could do." She adds quickly, "But don't you think for one moment that this has anything to do with me. God caused all of this to happen. Every bit of it. We're just doing what he has led us to do."[1]

Little wonder that many visitors to Brookwood depart with the feeling that they have just discovered a place on earth where angels reside.

Our son's job is to help produce some seventy thousand poinsettia plants each year. Recently, Grant talked excitedly about his job. We listened intently and praised him. Then we took the opportunity to raise another topic: helping him to identify his purpose in life.

"We're proud of the job you are doing for Brookwood," I said, "but we also want you to think about your job for God."

"Job for God? What's that?" he asked.

"We have jobs we go to every day, where we get paid to do something or make something; but our job for God is what we decide we can do with our individual talents for God."

After some discussion, Grant determined that because he loves to sing and is good at it, he should use his music to "help others feel good."

"That's a wonderful job for God," we agreed.

We thought about that conversation as we read this letter from one of the world's most famous angels: Roma Downey. She played the lead angel on the popular TV series *Touched by an Angel*, seen in ninety million homes every week during the 1990s.

She writes that, one day, she was given a clearer understanding about *her* job for God.

The Job of an Angel

As the angel Monica on *Touched by an Angel*, my Irish heart was always warmed knowing that every episode reflected biblical truths—primarily, that here on earth, we entertain angels unawares.

My fellow cast members and I also came to understand, early on in the development of the series, that our roles would extend past that of on-air angels to off-air as well—where we were called to channel God's grace.

One day I was visiting a children's hospital, trying to do my part in bringing a ray of hope to little ones and their hurting families. As I walked down a corridor, I encountered nurses accompanying a bereaved family from a room. Glancing beyond them, I could see the form of a lifeless child lying on the bed.

The mother's face was contorted in pain and anguish. My heart cried out to her. For an instant, our eyes met. I watched her expression transform into a look of hope—indicating that she knew exactly who I was.

"I prayed that you would come," said the woman with whispered urgency. "I asked God to send me an angel to confirm that my child is in heaven. And here you are."

I wanted to say, "No . . . you're wrong. I'm not really an angel . . . I'm an actress who plays an angel." But my lips failed to move. I looked deeply into those reddened eyes, above the tear-streaked cheeks of a grieving mother, and chose to say nothing.

Instead, I placed an arm around her and whispered, "Let me pray with you."

Standing there in the hospital corridor, we prayed. Words of comfort flowed from my lips, but surely, they were not from me—they were words bathed by the grace of God.

Then, with my hands extending to the mother's shoulders, I smiled tenderly and said, "God be with you."

Wiping away a tear that had formed at the corner of her eye, she expressed deep-felt gratitude. "Thank you, thank you so much."

Yet I left the hospital wearing a heavy cloak of guilt. I felt I had somehow done the wrong thing. That I had allowed myself to become an actor on the stage of *real* life . . . leading a mourning mother to believe I was something that I was not.

As soon as I could, I telephoned my dear friend, fellow actor, and confidant, Della Reese. She was the one I always turned to for words of encouragement.

"I feel like such a fraud," I said into the phone after explaining what had happened.

"Why would you feel like that?" she asked compassionately.

"Because that poor woman was in a vulnerable place and needed support . . . thinking that God had sent *me* there to provide it for her."

"And who says he didn't?" said Della matter-of-factly. Then, with calm authority, she added, "Baby, there are times when *we* need to step out of the way, and let God use us to channel his grace."

What was clear to me on that day was that God had winked.
Yes, he channeled grace through me, but he had also channeled
wisdom through my friend Della Reese.

Roma Downey

Discovering that her role as an angel extended beyond the script and the TV cameras was, for Roma, the revelation of her job for God—her greater purpose for Him.

God calls us to be his ambassadors. Sometimes that means He needs us to be a Godwink Link—the courier of a godwink—in the lives of others to let them know that they are not alone. Often it is simply to pray with someone in need.

Ask God to help you become more attuned to his voice. Is there someone he wants you to reach out to today, as his angel on earth, with a message of love and hope? Is there a way you can use the unique talents He has given you to serve His purpose?

> *Let your light shine before others,*
> *that they may see your good deeds*
> *and glorify your Father in heaven.*
> Matthew 5:16 NIV

Roma went to the hospital that day to help uplift others, but as a bonus, she received a great blessing herself: greater clarity about her job for God—her purpose.

Dear friends, let us love one another,
because love comes from God.
Whoever loves is a child of God
and knows God.

1 John 4:7 GNT

4

How Can I Overcome My Terrible Feelings of Anxiety?

*Cast all your anxieties on him
because he cares for you.*

1 Peter 5:7 NIV

We want answers!

We need to know that our families are safe; that we won't be downsized; or that we'll have enough in the checking account to make it through the month. We crave clear answers when we get a scary medical report and have to wait days or weeks for an outcome. And we long for decisive answers in our relationships.

"I'd almost rather have the answer of bad news," said

one friend, awaiting a biopsy. "At least I could get started on dealing with it. The uncertainty is killing me with anxiety!"

Difficult times are when we especially need to get connected to our faith. We need to believe that our lives are not random; that we're not like twigs floating down a stream to destinations unknown. We want to know that there is a purpose for everything we're going through; that someone is really up there watching over us and that He knows what's going on, even if we don't. We want to know that this lonely feeling we have is false—that we are never alone, that we're on His GPS . . . God's Positioning System.

During times of trouble, we should be on the lookout for godwinks. That's one way for God to communicate with us. In fact, one of the best things about godwinks is that they are like a handrail along your way, giving you hope when answers are not forthcoming . . . assuring you that everything is going to be okay.

As Krista pours out her heart in this letter, we can feel her yearning for answers.

Moe—the Rest of the Story

About six months ago, I was in one of the worst states in my life. I was recently divorced, I had a horrible boss to contend with at work, and I wasn't speaking to my parents. I was becoming a hermit, miserable and sinking deeper every day.

One day I was talking with my chiropractor about life, how

hard it is, and that I just felt hopeless. At the end of my appointment, she handed me a slip of paper on which she had written, "*God Winks, God Winks on Love, God Winks at You*, by SQuire Rushnell." She added, "Whenever I'm feeling down, I read these books."

For the next week, I read several of your stories each night. I began to feel like a huge burden was being lifted. I felt better and was even able to smile! I was seeing the light at the end of the tunnel and believed I really was going to get through this . . . whatever "this" was.

Out of the blue, my mother called, wanting to get together to talk and reconcile. If she'd called ten days earlier, I would have refused . . . but now I was able to face the music, make amends, and have amends made to me. It was beautiful.

That night, thanking God and smiling, I opened up one of your books and read about Moe.

Author's note:

Krista is referring to the story I called "A Mutt Named Moe," told by actor Chuck McCann about the day he nearly struck a black Labrador with his truck, then chased the dog down to see if it was all right. Here are some excerpts:

The dog jumped into the truck right next to Chuck and later accompanied his new best friend as he plastered posters around the neighborhood: "Found: small black Lab."

The next day, Chuck received a phone call. A

lady said the dog sounded like a mutt that she, too, had once found and returned to its owner. She had a number. Chuck called it, leaving a message saying that he may have found their dog.

Six days passed.

Finally, a woman telephoned. "Yes, that sounds like our dog," she said in an unemotional, monotone voice. "We were moving to a new house. He was playing in the yard and must have run off."

"What's his name?" asked Chuck, with a slight trace of annoyance that the woman had no expression of concern.

"Moe."

Chuck turned from the phone and yelled, "Moe!"

At that instant, the happy, tail-wagging black Lab dashed into the room.

"Yep. That's your dog," said Chuck. "Didn't you get my message from last week?"

"Ye-e-sss," said the woman with some hesitancy, "but we were moving, and I thought he'd be all right where he was."

Chuck stared at the phone.

"Ma'am, if you don't want the dog, I'll keep him."

"All right," she said.

That was how Moe came to be Chuck's permanent best friend. They were inseparable. Everywhere Chuck went, Moe went. And Moe always had his favorite spot in the truck—right next to Chuck.

They were best pals for ten years.

Then, one day, Moe seemed to be out of sorts. He wasn't his normal, friendly, frisky self. Instead of jumping up when Chuck came into the room, he'd lay there. Sad looking.

"What's the matter, Moe boy? We've got to get you to the doctor."

"It's a stomach disorder," explained the vet. "All we can do is prescribe a medication to try to prevent the disease from spreading."

A while later . . . tears welling in his eyes . . . Chuck sadly cradled Moe in his arms and watched as his best friend went to sleep. And never woke up.

Ten months passed, and Chuck was in a park . . . where a dog show was going on, with rescue groups looking for new homes for their animals. As he passed a booth featuring Lhasa apsos, one particular pup came right up to Chuck.

"He's like a small bag of feathers," said Chuck with a tone of surprise, lifting the tiny dog with soft fur and a face that belonged on a stuffed toy.

The dog had one blue eye and one brown.

"This is the cutest dog I've ever seen," said Chuck to a lady with the rescue group. "What's his name?"

"Moe."

The world stopped. Or so it seemed. Chuck was astonished.

"What did you say?"

"His name is Moe," she repeated.

Chuck couldn't believe his ears.

"I . . . I've got to have this dog," he said, promising to provide a wonderful home for the little creature.

The story ended with Chuck saying, "I'll always miss my first Moe . . . but this little Moe is filling a big hole in my heart."

Back to Krista's letter . . .

I finished that story with uncontrollable tears flooding my face. You see, almost to the day, our 105-pound yellow Labrador retriever, Jaeger, had also passed away. He was the most beautiful, sweetest, most lovable dog on earth. He brought so much joy, not only to my family, but also to many others. He was truly special.

The next day, I called my mother and asked her if I could stop by after work. I brought your books and waited for my dad to get home. I opened up to the story about Moe and read it aloud.

I barely got through it. In my life, I have had only a few glimpses of my father crying. This time I got more than a glimpse—he wept. My mother was sobbing, and by the end, there was a sort of *wow* feeling at how God lets us know He is there, guiding us and taking care of us. We just have to be ready and listen.

After that day, my parents would wake up every morning, have their devotions, and read your book. We'd get on the phone and talk about them. Even now, my dad calls and asks, "What was your godwink today?"

Thank you again for writing your stories. They have truly touched the lives of me and my family.

Krista Clark

If someone asks you, "What was your godwink today?" feel good about it. That person—like Krista's dad—may be using godwinks as a point of reference, recognizing that godwinks come from a loving God who cares enough to send a reassuring message directly to you.

Just as you would return a phone call or email received from a friend or family member, a godwink is an invitation for you to get back in touch with Him—through prayer, of course.

Do not be anxious about anything,
but in everything by prayer and
supplication with thanksgiving
let your requests be made known to God.
And the peace of God,
which surpasses all understanding,
will guard your hearts and your minds in
Christ Jesus.

Philippians 4:6–7 ESV

5

I Feel Alone, Without a Friend

Encourage one another
and build each other up.

1 Thessalonians 5:11 NIV

Most of us, at one time or another, have felt as though we were the only person on the planet with our particular problem.

Perhaps you have a fear of public speaking. As you look around at others in a crowded room, everyone seems glib and perfectly at ease. You begin to panic, thinking, "Oh, no, they might call on me to speak!" You picture an embarrassing outcome, convinced that if you're asked to speak, you'll stutter like a fool.

Whatever the cause of your fear or loneliness, it's an awful place to be.

As with most discomforts like this, the sooner we can pull ourselves under the protective arm of God—much the way we hid under our mother's apron as a child or crawled onto our father's lap—the sooner the sense of vulnerability will begin to dissipate.

Yet, as much as you think your problem is unique—whatever it is—you'd be hard-pressed to top Cheryn's challenge. Here's her story.

The Dilemma of Hair Pullers

Since the age of twelve, I've suffered from a condition called trichotillomania–in layman's terms, compulsive hair pulling.

When I was growing up, no one, including my doctor, knew how to help. I was alone. I suffered great shame, believing I'd brought the affliction upon myself. I felt powerless. No matter how hard I tried, it seemed that my hands had a mind of their own. "What's wrong with me?" I'd often wonder.

It was tough being a teen. Sometimes people rudely inquired about my lack of eyelashes and eyebrows. I was lonely. I kept people at a safe distance. But every night, I'd pray for wisdom and for God to send someone who understood.

At age twenty-five, I read a letter in *Ask Ann Landers* from a mom whose child suffered from compulsive hair pulling. I was astounded! It meant that I was not alone. "Ann Landers" pointed out that more than a million people suffered from this syndrome. It even had a medical name. At that moment, my journey toward healing began. I took small steps at first, telling only a few friends of my condition. Some expressed disgust, but others tried to understand.

Then, one day, God winked.

I reside in the lightly populated rural area of Soquel, California. A friend called to say she'd just met a woman like me—with trich. Her name was Christina, and my friend gave me her phone number. I quickly dialed, a sweet voice answered, and from the first moment, Christina and I chatted like old friends.

We were thrilled to find someone else who knew our pain—someone who understood. We talked of meeting soon, but in the meantime, Christina said, "I want to mail you some literature."

I gave her my address. She let out a piercing scream.

It turns out, we live only two houses away from each other!

We immediately dropped our phones and, in the dark of night, ran outside in our pajamas, hugged, jumped, and cried.

When we walked back to my house and into the light, Christina slowly lifted her long hair, revealing patchy, bald spots. Then, with a deep breath, I took off my makeup and let her see me as no one else ever had—not even my husband of ten years. In that moment, I knew my childhood prayer had been answered. I was not alone. Through that miraculous godwink, I felt as though I'd met my long-lost twin, someone who understood my pain and struggles.

We talked for hours. Christina shared her dream to open a

trich learning center, and I told her my thoughts of writing a book about my lonely experience.

Since then, Christina went on to open that trichotillomania center, where tens of thousands have found help. And I wrote not just one but two books: *You Are Not Alone—Compulsive Hair Pulling, the Enemy Within* and *What's Happening to My Child? A Guide for Parents of Hair Pullers.*

That's what happens when God winks at you!

Cheryn Salazar

What a classic case of Divine Alignment—a thesis I've written about in another book—how invisible threads seem to have reached across time and space and in this case, through an amazing godwink, connected two lonely people with a rare disorder.

The moment Christina and Cheryn discovered that they were neighbors, divinely placed on the same street, a lifelong friendship was born. God knew they needed each other, could identify with each other's challenges, and would team up to be a powerful force in showing kindness and compassion to others.

Sometimes just knowing that we are not suffering alone gives us hope to continue on in spite of our struggles.

In the Bible, the apostle Peter asks this of us:

> *Be ye all likeminded, compassionate,*
> *loving as brethren,*

tenderhearted, humbleminded.
1 Peter 3:8 ASV

God will help you get through the difficult, fearful, and lonely days in your life—and when you trust in Him, you will even triumph in spite of those tough times.

6

If Someone Is in Trouble, Should I Stop to Help?

If anyone has the world's goods
and sees his brother in need,
yet closes his heart against him,
how does God's love abide in him?

1 John 3:17 ESV

How often have you seen a news story about a person who was obviously in trouble, yet people, not wanting to get involved, walked right on by?

Jesus told a similar parable about a man who was beaten and robbed and left to die on the street. Two people passed him by. Then a third, a fellow from Samaria, stopped to help.

"A Samaritan . . . bandaged his wounds . . . brought him

to an inn and took care of him," said Jesus. "Which of these three do you think was a neighbor?"

"He who showed mercy," someone answered.

Then Jesus said, "Go and do likewise."[1]

That parable came to mind as I read a letter from Steve Hartman in Arizona.

The Cabbie and the Kidney

There's a godwink story that recently got all the folks here in Phoenix talking.

Tom Chappell is a cab driver. He doesn't get lost very often, but one day a few months ago, he was a little late picking up his fare, Rita Van Loenen. And Rita was not happy. In fact, she was downright cranky and didn't give him a tip.

So over the next few months, every time Rita called a cab, which driver do you think showed up at her house? Tom. You see, Tom's the type of guy who wants to learn as much as he can about why people are the way they are—why they are unhappy with their lot in life.

Tom noticed that he always took Rita to the same address—a medical facility with the name Southwest Kidney Dialysis on the door. He figured that whatever was going on behind that door was probably a big part of the reason Rita was miserable.

He became more curious and found out that what she really needed was a kidney transplant—and that finding a perfect match is like finding a needle in a haystack. None of her family or friends fit the bill.

So Tom offered to get tested himself.

Rita was so touched by his offer that her stone demeanor cracked. When he actually went through with it, she was blown away. And when the test results came back, they both were in awe. If the match had been any closer, they would have been siblings.

Then, sad news. Doctors at Mayo Clinic determined that Tom had other medical issues. Despite his best intentions, it was too risky for him to be a donor.

Mayo Clinic spokesperson said, "There is no doubting that Tom Chappell's heart was in the right place; it's just a matter of his kidneys."

Well, as you can imagine, Tom took the news hard. He felt he was letting Rita down. He insisted to the doctors, "God sent me a message. The man upstairs wants me to do this!" He reminded them that he'd even quit smoking in anticipation of being accepted as Van Loenen's donor.

But it wasn't to be.

What happened to Rita? As of this writing, she's still on the waiting list for a donor. But she hopes that all the publicity (the story got local newspaper and television coverage) will help her find the right match. Meanwhile, Rita says she thinks Tom is taking the news about his not being able to donate his kidney "a bit harder than I am."

There was one good godwink for Tom, though. You see, a daughter he had not heard from in thirty years happened to catch the story on TV. She immediately made the connection that they were talking about the father she had lost so long ago when her parents went through a difficult divorce.

"When I got that phone call," says Tom, ". . . when the voice on the other end said, 'This is your daughter,' . . . I went right to the floor and wept."

Tom's boss arranged for him to fly to Nashville so father and daughter could reunite.

"When I saw her," said Tom, "we were like two magnets coming together."

He's still sorry he couldn't help Rita, but he sometimes wonders if maybe getting his family back together was what God had in mind all along.

"If I died this second," he says, "I could not be happier. I got my daughter and my three beautiful grandchildren."

Steve Hartman

Imagine yourself in Tom's shoes, driving his cab.

You get a call to pick up a woman who turns out to be grumpy.

Instead of giving her attitude, you decide you're going to act like you think Jesus might act if He were driving the cab. You suspend judgment and instead feel compassion for Rita. Then, upon learning she needs a kidney and that a donor hasn't been found, you get *yourself* tested and find you are the perfect match. You talk it over with God, and He tells you to go ahead . . . offer your kidney to the grumpy customer who gave you no tip.

Can you or I imagine ourselves displaying that kind of altruism?

Notwithstanding the medical risks Tom would have gladly taken—which, in the end, doctors deemed too high—God was directing Tom to step up and help someone in need.

God expects us to treat others with kindness, grace, and mercy because God did that for us. And when we help others, God gives us favor—the way He blessed Tom, reuniting him with a long-lost daughter.

> *Give, and it will be given to you.*
> *A good measure, pressed down,*
> *shaken together and running over,*
> *will be poured into your lap.*
> *For with the measure you use,*
> *it will be measured to you.*
>
> Luke 6:38 NIV

As Jesus said, "Go and do likewise."

7

Will God Really Provide for All My Needs?

My God will meet all your needs
according to his glorious riches in Christ Jesus.
Philippians 4:19 NIV

As much as you like to prepare for the unexpected—diligently saving up for a rainy day and stocking up for harsh winters—you also know that, from time to time, life will unleash a storm you never anticipated.

And when it does, you'd better hope your "prayer tank" is full. For in times like these, getting by will be only by God's grace.

This letter from Shannon Firth Williams illustrates the desperate feeling you might have when, on a beautiful day and everything seems to be in perfect order, suddenly an emergency comes upon you. When that happens, your human mind may be incapable of formulating reasonable solutions. Those are the times God intervenes, with a wink.

Stranded by Summer Snow

It was a typical July day in north-central Washington. I was fourteen; my family and I had been camping and fishing for the weekend, and we were returning home. Due to the nice weather, we weren't in a hurry, so my dad suggested we take the long route.

The "long route" consisted of going over a mountain pass, adding about one hour to our trip time. I thought it was a great idea, as did my mother, and it didn't matter to my infant sister and little cousin.

As we started up the pass, we discovered the gate had been pulled closed. Inasmuch as it was the middle of July and the heat index was about 102 degrees, my father thought the closed gate must have been a prank. So he opened the gate, and we proceeded on our way. About thirty minutes into the drive, we came to a tree that had fallen across the road. My father and I got out of the car and pulled the tree aside far enough for us to drive around.

Continuing up the pass, we noticed that the winter snows had not completely melted in the shady areas: a little ice and snow remained. We laughed about the stubborn nature of the snow and delighted in the "winter" treat.

At the three-quarters mark, we encountered snow on the road, and it quickly became a problem. My father is nothing if not stubborn, so he elected to persevere and prove that he was mightier than the mountain. Besides, we were running low on gasoline, and he concluded that we did not have enough to retrace our steps. Within a few minutes, we came to a fork in the road. One path went up a steep incline. The other was blocked by more fallen trees. As we started up the hill, we lost traction and got stuck. My father gunned the engine in an effort to get us unstuck, which used up most of the remaining fuel.

Stranded on a pass that was closed, we knew we couldn't expect a vehicle to rescue us. We took inventory of what we had for supplies to survive a night in what was sure to be freezing—yes, it was cold up on the pass—temperatures.

We had consumed most of the food Mom had packed for the weekend. A few potato chips, one piece of fried chicken, and some fruit were all that remained. My mother, after years of trying, had stopped smoking . . . and carrying matches. Only one was left in the packet. We had sleeping bags but no warm clothing.

In sum, we were in trouble and not sure what to do.

My father had turned off the engine, hoping to conserve the gallon or so of remaining gas in case he had to build a large fire to signal rescuers.

I had gotten out of the van, trying to help push our way out of the snow, and then decided to take a walk back down to the fork. I wondered how far it was to the nearest civilization. I was an athlete and in good condition. I knew I could walk a long way, perhaps far enough to get help. But I was scared and said a prayer asking for God's guidance.

As I stood in the middle of the fork, a glint caught my attention. I walked toward it. About one hundred feet down the road and twenty-five feet to the side was a shiny, red, five-gallon gas can. It was full! The can was sitting under a pine tree, yet there was not one pine needle, water spot, or speck of dirt on it . . . as if it had just been placed there for us.

I ran back to my father and mother and told them what I had found. It seemed incredible, and they ran down the road to confirm my findings. We all were amazed.

We filled our gas tank, got the van unstuck and turned around, and retraced our earlier steps. We tried to rationalize that the gas can had perhaps been left by someone working for the forestry department, but given its like-new condition and the impassable conditions of the roads, we felt it unlikely that anyone had been up that mountain all summer. Every explanation we could think of was discounted as unlikely or impossible.

I know that God winked at my family that day and possibly saved our lives. For it was through the grace of God and his love for us that we were able to make it off the mountain.

The gasoline we found was just enough—and I mean just

enough—to get us back to civilization. We coasted into town and
filled up our tank, thanking God all the way.

Shannon Firth Williams

Shannon's family had just enough gas to get to a safe place. Isn't that just like God?

Can you imagine the desperation everyone must have felt, trapped in a forest with no way out? Shannon's father was most likely quietly blaming himself for getting them into such a mess. And Shannon's mind must have been swimming in "what ifs" as she walked back to the fork in the road.

But this young teenager did the right thing. First, she took a step of faith by "doing something"—taking a walk. Second, she asked God for help.

The family was amazed by the way God came to their rescue, but who wouldn't be . . . a shiny new gas can, full to the brim, out there in the wilderness? The experience solidified Shannon's belief in God and had another side benefit. Her parents, who until then were not believers, began attending church right after that, and still do.

> Listen! It's the voice of someone shouting,
> "Clear the way through the wilderness for
>   the Lord!"
>
> Isaiah 40:3

This is a good time for each of us to check the gauge on our own prayer tank. Is it approaching empty? Why not store up for those unexpected emergencies that are sure to happen by filling up every day? And, through faith, let us rest assured that God will provide, in all situations.

> *The LORD is my shepherd,*
> *I shall not be in want.*
>
> Psalm 23:1 NIV

Oh, by the way, the Gaelic meaning of *Shannon* is "God is gracious."

8

Will I Ever Find My Perfect Mate?

I waited patiently for the LORD;
he turned to me and heard my cry.

Psalm 40:1 NIV

How many movies and books are love stories—all about boy meets girl? How many songs are about falling in love?

During our teenage years, love was always on our minds, and it continues to be a significant factor in our adult lives.

JP was becoming resigned to the notion that finding God's perfect mate for her was just another unfulfilled wish. She began to wonder if her dreams to settle down with a wonderful guy were nothing more than a fairy tale. She writes about it in her letter.

Don't Change the Color of Your Hair

I had been single for ten-plus years and was actually getting rather comfortable in that role, even though my family and friends were always trying to fix me up.

After making many poor choices in boyfriends, I had become tired of the dating life; yet I didn't want to spend my life alone. While reading *When God Winks on Love*, I decided to do what I read in one of your stories: ask God to find my soul mate—my *bashert*, as they say in Yiddish. "I might as well ask God to find him," I joked. "After all, he has a better view!"

So in October 2006, I decided to let God be in charge. I basically forgot about dating.

Three months later, a guy I knew just as an acquaintance was driving by my place of work and noticed a fire behind the building I was in. He ran into the building and basically rescued me from the fire.

A couple weeks later, he gave me a Valentine's Day card and wrote, "Don't change the color of your hair . . . I love you just the way you are!"

"Wow, kind of intense," I thought. But I ignored the message, since I wasn't the least bit interested in him. He was just a nice, kind, caring, humorous, and intelligent man. That was as far as it went.

The next morning, I awoke to the words written on my valentine blaring from my clock radio: "Don't change the color of your hair . . . I love you just the way you are!" It was a song I'd never paid attention to before: "Just the Way You Are" by Billy Joel. I jumped up and ran to find the card to confirm that the words were the same.

They were! My thoughts were a jumble: "Is this a godwink? I think so. Oh no, what does this mean?"

A short while later, a friend asked if I knew whether this person was available—because she wanted to fix him up with her friend. That question, surprisingly, sparked a little fire of jealousy in me. "Hey, he's flirting with *me*—he's *mine*," I thought. But . . . did I even want him?

Well, to bring this story to its happy ending, God *did* find my soul mate—just as I had asked—and gave me several godwinks to keep me on the path to marriage. Now, five years later, I'm happier and more in love than I ever dreamed possible!

JP

Don't we love happy endings? God wants us to have a mate. He said it himself, when he created Adam:

> *It is not good for the man to be alone.*
> *I will make a helper who is just right*
> *for him.*

Genesis 2:18 NLT

Perhaps you know of someone who has endured one bad relationship after another looking for that perfect mate. (No . . . I wasn't talking about *you*, of course.)

The truth is, when we get impatient, we're more likely to jump into the wrong relationship, missing the true love of our lives that God wants to arrange through Divine Alignment.

I probably don't need to tell you the "wrong choice" stats. They're not pretty:

The divorce rate in America for first marriages is 41 percent; for second marriages, 60 percent; and for third marriages, 73 percent.[1]

Yikes!

Yet on the other side of the coin are many wonderful marriages that seem to have been made in heaven. Those are the couples we should look to, to learn what *they* have done *right*.

In the ancient Scriptures, God laid out the boundaries of an ideal relationship:

> *Love is patient and kind. Love is not*
> *jealous or boastful or proud or rude. It*
> *does not demand its own way. It is not*
> *irritable, and it keeps no record of being*
> *wronged. It does not rejoice about injustice*
> *but rejoices whenever the truth wins out.*
> *Love never gives up, never loses faith, is*
> *always hopeful, and endures through every*
> *circumstance.*
>
> 1 Corinthians 13:4–7 NLT

If every couple followed those guidelines—which are just as relevant today as when they were written more than two thousand years ago—imagine how the divorce statistics would change.

In *When God Winks on Love*, I offered a yardstick for my daughters Robin and Hilary to use in "measuring" admirers. It's a tool that can work for everyone.

If a person has all of the following qualities, chances are, you have found your ideal mate:

L: Laughter	Do you laugh when you're together? It releases tension.
A: Appreciation	Is there a frequent expression of appreciation? It's essential.
U: Understanding	Does he or she not merely *hear* but *understand* what you say?
G: God	Do you pray together? God *must* be front and center in your relationship.
H: Honor	Will you hold each other in higher honor than you hold yourselves?
S: Support	Are you confident that he or she will always be watching your back?

If both partners have all six of those attributes, it is much more likely that you will have a heavenly marriage . . . with lots of L-A-U-G-H-S.

If your problem is that you simply haven't found anyone with whom you want to spend the rest of your life, guard yourself against sinking into desperation. If you do feel desperate, then you may not be truly seeking God's guidance. When you trust God completely, the unpleasant feelings of desperation will be replaced by peace and contentment in being where you are in your life. You may even decide, as JP had at the beginning of her story, that being single isn't all that bad. You can feel confident that, in God's time, if it is His will, you will be divinely aligned with your perfect mate.

When that time comes, it is critical for you and your partner to enter into a trinity with God—three as one—by committing to pray together starting with as little as five minutes a day. In our book *Couples Who Pray*, we show through story after story that prayer is a mortar for your marriage. If you pray together, you will never fall out of love—in fact, your love will grow stronger.

JP said in her letter, "I'm happier and more in love than I ever dreamed possible."

You can be too.

9

God Never Forgets!

I will not forget you! See, I have
engraved you on the palms of my hands.
Isaiah 49:15–16 NIV

You forget things. I forget things.

We joke about it.

With a giggle a woman tells her friend, "I'm lucky I haven't lost my memory!" She knocks on wood, then promptly tilts her head and quips, "Who's there?"

A man answers his own question: "Do I believe in the hereafter? Absolutely! I walk into a room and say, 'What am I here after?'"

From time to time, we all forget.

God never does.

Perhaps a desire was planted in your heart when you were a child—something you wanted, something you aspired to—and over the years it faded from your memory . . . but not God's. He never forgets.

This letter from Jonna Fitzgerald underscores that.

The 45 RPM

When I was a little girl growing up during the 1960s and '70s, it was a tradition to watch the Miss Texas or Miss America pageants on TV. Playing pageant was a frequent pastime for me, and even though I was shy, I would produce mini-pageants on my front porch, complete with talent competition.

In 1973 a beautiful young woman named Judy Mallett was crowned Miss Texas. Judy's talent was playing the fiddle, and I was enthralled by her beauty and charisma. That was the moment I, at age nine, decided I *must* learn to play the fiddle so I could become Miss Texas—maybe even Miss America.

When school began that fall, a flyer was handed out announcing a new program called Mini Strings: a teacher would come to the school two mornings a week to teach violin. I promptly informed my mother that I would be taking violin lessons at school.

About the same time, my mom learned that Judy Mallett, the fiddle-playing Miss Texas, would be performing just a couple hours' drive from our home in Tyler. So Mom surprised me with a trip to see her.

After the program, there was a long line of people waiting for autographs. As a painfully shy child, it was a huge feat for me to stand in that line. But I was determined to meet my idol. As I got closer, I realized that she was autographing 45 rpm records featuring her fiddle performance of "Orange Blossom Special." How exciting!

When it was my turn to meet Judy, this introverted child blurted out, "I'm learning to play the fiddle and want to be Miss Texas, just like you."

Judy smiled and encouraged me to practice hard, and maybe I would get there.

Then she looked at me sadly and said, "I'm so sorry. I've just given out my last record." She shook her head, adding, "I don't have any more."

I was very disappointed. But I did walk away with an autographed photo and the knowledge that Miss Texas herself had just told me that if I practiced, I could be Miss Texas too.

So I practiced. And in 1985, I was blessed with the honor of being crowned Miss Texas. Imagine that. Another fiddle-playing Miss Texas!

The following year was the Texas Sesquicentennial, so I made many personal appearances, including a booking by a bank owner who reserved a date in December for me to perform at his annual employee-appreciation Christmas party.

Believe me, a year as Miss Texas is the next-best thing to getting a PhD in human relations. You learn to live out of a suitcase, meet many people, and encounter all types of situations—some of which were challenging for a formerly bashful young woman from a small town in East Texas. Sometimes I would make appearances in three or four cities in a single day and would lose track of where I was.

As December approached and I became road weary, my prayers increasingly took the form of asking God, Why is this so tough? What is it that I am supposed to learn from this turmoil?

When I finally arrived at the long-ago booked Bank Employee Appreciation Day, the bank owner's wife met me with a warm greeting. She then told me that her husband had passed away just a couple weeks before but had been adamant that the celebration for his employees be held just as it was every year.

When it came time for the widow to give out gifts, she called me to the stage.

"My husband personally wrapped a gift for you several months before he died," she said with a smile. "He asked me to be certain that Miss Texas received this package."

As I opened the beautifully wrapped box, it became evident that God had a hand in it. Imagine my astonishment to find that inside the box was an autographed 45 rpm record of Judy Mallett, Miss Texas 1973, playing "Orange Blossom Special" on her fiddle!

God used a man I'd never met, a man who knew almost nothing about me, to send me a godwink, and it profoundly changed my life.

By connecting a childhood incident of momentary disappointment with the remarkable gift from a man I will meet only in the next lifetime, God let me know that he had placed me exactly where he'd planned for me to be all along. My heavenly Father

knew that I was to be Miss Texas long before I ever knew it,
and he sent me that godwink just to let me know.

Jonna Fitzgerald

The disappointment of a little girl was buried deeply in Jonna's heart. She really wanted that "Orange Blossom Special" 45 rpm from her Miss Texas hero. Over the years, that disappointment faded into a distant memory. But God never forgot. He knew that the gift she had hoped to receive as a young girl would have a much more powerful meaning for her at a later time and place. That time was after Jonna had traveled down countless roads and had begun to feel disillusioned and weary. She questioned her purpose—what was it all for? What was she supposed to learn?

> *Who knows but that you*
> *have come to your royal position*
> *for such a time as this?*
>
> Esther 4:14 NIV

Yet as soon as Jonna opened that special gift, she knew exactly what she had learned: that God's magnificent hand was guiding her every step along every path.

> *A gift opens the way*
> *and ushers the giver*
> *into the presence of the great.*
>
> Proverbs 18:16 NIV

We live life forward but so often understand it backward.

You cannot see all that God has planned for you. But you can trust that He holds your future in His hands and that He has a plan to guide your steps and light your path.

> *Trust in the LORD with all your heart,*
> *and lean not on your own understanding;*
> *in all your ways acknowledge Him,*
> *and He shall direct your paths.*
>   Proverbs 3:5–6 NKJV

Whenever you think God has forgotten about you, remember Jonna's story. He didn't forget the desires in the heart of that little girl. He won't forget yours, either.

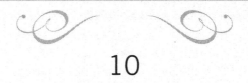

10

Can Laughter Help Relieve My Pain?

We were filled with laughter,
and we sang for joy.

Psalm 126:2 NLT

A widely reported study by the University of Chicago claims that having a good sense of humor can add eight years to your life.[1] That's no surprise to those of us who remember the famous *Reader's Digest* section "Laughter, the Best Medicine."

Mayo Clinic confirms the finding. They say that laughter "stimulates your heart, lungs and muscles, and increases the endorphins that are released by your brain." Further, laughter can "stimulate circulation and aid muscle relaxation, both of which help reduce some of the physical symptoms of stress." If you are suffering pain, the clinic suggests: "Laughter may ease pain by causing the body to produce its own natural painkillers."[2]

Of course, when you are in the middle of a medical emergency, as Bonnie and her son were, laughing is the last thing you want to do. It turns out . . . it *was* the last thing they did.

This, Too, Shall Pass

My twenty-one-year-old son was taken to the emergency room in a tremendous amount of pain.

On my way to the hospital, I started praying. I asked God to show us favor: that my son would be taken into treatment immediately; that the doctors would make a quick diagnosis and ease his pain.

I chose a route to the hospital that led past a church, where the message on the marquee caught my attention—but would make sense only later on.

In the emergency room, God did indeed show us favor. My son was taken to triage immediately; the nurses saw how much pain he was in and put us in the last treatment room available; and the doctor promptly diagnosed my son's crisis. He said he was suffering from a kidney stone that needed to pass through his system.

Right then and there, I knew that the message on the church

marquee had been a humorous wink from God. It had read: "This, too, shall pass"!

Bonnie Bickerstaff

Bonnie was so relieved to see her son out of pain that she couldn't help giggling as the image of that sign came back to mind.

We can be certain her son wasn't laughing as he was trying to pass the kidney stone. Ouch! Every second of pain must have seemed like an eternity.

If you are immersed in a painful trial today, wondering whether you can endure one more minute, there *is* a light at the end of the tunnel. That light is Jesus.

I am the light of the world.

John 8:12 KJV

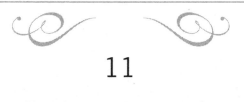

11

I Feel So Unimportant—Do I Matter?

See what great love the Father has lavished on us,
that we should be called children of God!

1 John 3:1 NIV

Have you ever traveled through the mountains, looked up, and thought, "Boy, am I small"?

I remember having that feeling as a nine-year-old on my first trip to New York City: standing on a crowded sidewalk, gazing up at the Empire State Building as hundreds of people rushed by, making me feel like an ant.

From the perspective of being just a tiny speck in the total pool of people on earth, it is hard not to wonder, "Do I matter? Can I make a difference?"

God has assignments for each of us that we don't know about and can't imagine. Kimberly, for instance, thought her only purpose on one trip was to participate in a bike hike across America. She shared what happened.

A Man Named Fred

In 1992, accompanied by fourteen friends, I rode my bicycle from Seattle, Washington, to Atlantic City, New Jersey, to benefit the American Lung Association. One day in Idaho, I decided to ride alone. My friends, and the van that usually followed us, were far ahead of me.

I was enjoying the day and the ride when, without warning, my bike broke down. A closer inspection revealed that the tiniest and most essential screw that holds the derailleur together was gone. Without a derailleur to shift through the gears, I could not ride my bike.

I looked around for help, but all I could see was a small town on a distant hill—a very long hill that I had just ridden down! So I began walking, uphill, pushing my broken bike. I was angry and scared and confused. I was only in Idaho, and I still had thousands of miles to go—this was not good!

I passed a sign identifying the town as Kamiah and, noting that the buildings lived up to the sign's description as "Western/Victorian," made my way to a car repair shop. I explained that I was a cyclist from New Jersey, riding my bike across the country, and I needed this small screw for the derailleur. The mechanic interrupted, "New Jersey?"

"That's right," I said.

"Wait until I tell Fred that you're here!" he said. "You have to meet him, he will be so glad to know you're here!"

I felt uneasy and wondered what in the world I had gotten myself into. Here I was, alone in the middle of Idaho with no cell phone, no money, a broken bicycle, my friends far away . . . and this overly eager man insisting I meet "Fred."

The mechanic decided the best place to find a screw as tiny as I needed was the sewing-machine shop. We walked there, and I explained my story to the owner while the mechanic went to tell Fred—whoever he was—that I had arrived.

Some twenty or thirty boxes of sewing-machine screws later, we found one that fit. As the owner walked me back to the automotive shop, she told me that when a stranger comes to a small town like this, with fewer than a thousand people, word of the new arrival travels fast.

Sure enough, as we left the shop, three people walked by, and one shouted, "Oh! You must be Kimberly! Fred will be so glad to see you!"

It crossed my mind that maybe I had entered a science-fiction world, some sort of twilight zone where I would spend the rest of my days, never to see my friends again.

Back at the repair shop, we put the sewing-machine screw into the derailleur, and it worked! I used the shop phone to call my friends and waited for them to pick me up.

Moments later, a van pulled up, and a frail, elderly man carrying two brown bags of vegetables got out. He walked into the shop and looked at me with wide eyes and a smile and said, "You must be Kimberly!"

I answered with a nervous smile, "You must be Fred."

As he walked toward me, I could see a strange sadness on his face. His voice shook as he said, "I am so glad to see you. I can't believe you're actually here."

Fred told me his story. Soon we realized we were from the same area near Flemington, New Jersey. It turned out that Fred had been good friends with some of my high school teachers, including my driving instructor and my running coach. Fred told me that he had left New Jersey suddenly twelve years ago because something hurtful had happened, and he could not bring himself to return. All of those years, he had been praying for forgiveness.

I felt compassion as Fred tried to hold back tears. He said, "I prayed that if someone came to this small town in the middle of Idaho who was from my home town in New Jersey, it would be a miracle and a sign that I had been forgiven."

In that moment I realized that God had a greater purpose for me—for all of us. I was stunned, and the importance of what had happened seemed enormous. Both Fred and I were speechless.

This story still holds tremendous power for me—especially on the days when I feel I'm doing poorly in some area of my life. I know that God has a purpose for all of us and is using us every day, in ways that we may never even know.

God will use *whatever* we have to give, and he will use it in a magnificent way to bless others, to bring his peace, and to show his love. He has already used you today—perhaps to offer a smile, a gift of forgiveness, a moment of caring, a word of encouragement, or in mysterious ways of which you are not aware. We are the bearers of God's grace.

Kimberly Borin

The tiny piece that went missing from Kimberly's bike was essential—it was necessary for the bike to operate, but it also was pivotal to God's mission. The missing piece led her to an unfamiliar town, but she had no idea that *she* was a missing piece in Fred's life. Her detour was a divinely aligned time and place to release him from his inability to forgive himself.

Isn't it extraordinary how God uses us as unwitting messengers to touch people's lives in special and personal ways?

In Christ we who are many form one body,
and each member belongs to all the others.
Romans 12:5 NIV

All kinds of people step in and out of our lives. They have a profound effect on us, and we on them. God uses each of us to help one another along the way—sometimes even people we've never met before. It just confirms that we are on a glorious GPS—God's Positioning System—and

His awesome stitching of the invisible threads of Divine Alignment is guiding each of our journeys through life.

Let's remember what Kimberly said in her letter: "God has already used you today—perhaps to offer a smile, a gift of forgiveness, a moment of caring, a word of encouragement, or in mysterious ways of which you are not aware."

You do matter. You make a difference.

12

When I'm in Trouble, Can I Count on God to Hear My Prayers?

You will seek me and find me
when you seek me with all your heart.
Jeremiah 29:13 NIV

Can you imagine starting a "rainy day" bank account the day your house gets flooded?

Nope. That's a bit late.

Yet don't we sometimes start putting prayer into our "prayer bank" only when we run into a crisis?

God may indeed reach out and answer your prayers in a crisis. But doesn't it make more sense to build up your prayer account with regular deposits, developing your relationship with God, your spiritual banker, daily? Instead of waiting until a crisis hits, consider budgeting your time to work in a few minutes of daily prayer deposits. You'll be amazed at the interest that accrues.

We all know that days will come when we look at the checkbook and say, "Uh-oh! I've got a problem here." M.K. wrote about the day she looked into her purse and was alarmed at her findings.

Prayer and Winks

My husband had to have both of his knees replaced. He was forced to retire from his job, and I had lost mine. We were on Social Security, and needless to say, money was extremely tight.

I was worried. I had just twelve dollars in my wallet—no, $12.16, to be exact—and was wondering how I was going to buy food, pay the mortgage, and heat the house. It was January, and we live in Vermont.

I decided to affirm that divine order was at work, even though things looked pretty dismal. As I normally do, I prayed.

When I came home from my husband's rehab session the next day, I brought in the mail—and there was my godwink: a check for $1,216 from the mortgage company! Hundred-fold what was in my wallet. Apparently the company had taken out too much for our property taxes.

This godwink helped me get through a difficult time. We are still on Social Security, but my husband is back on track and has started a knife- and tool-sharpening business, which is growing a bit each month.

Who says there's no God? This omnipotent Spirit is part of you and will bring you through your trials.

M.K.

God is never late . . . but sometimes, I think just to let us know it's Him at work, He sure cuts it close. There was M.K., down to her last few dollars. She prayed. Or, more to the point, you could say that she spoke with the head of her bank: God. His funds never fall short. He supplies *all* of M.K.'s needs and your needs. Because she turned matters over to him and chose to rely on His support, her prayer was answered and she was provided for abundantly—an amazing godwink.

Here's something else to think about. Only human beings have a problem relying on God for provision. No other creature has this trouble. Jesus reminded us of that:

> *Look at the birds of the air;*
> *they do not sow or reap or store away in*
> *   barns,*
> *and yet your heavenly Father feeds them.*
> *Are you not much more valuable than they?*
>   Matthew 6:26 NIV

God runs a spiritual supermarket, open 24/7. It supplies *all* your needs. It is a storehouse filled with bountiful blessings for you. As a matter of fact, the ancient Scriptures say it's overflowing!

> *Ask and it will be given to you;*
> *seek and you will find;*
> *knock and the door will be opened to you.*
> Matthew 7:7 NIV

13

Will God Deliver Me from the Pain of My Childhood?

He will wipe every tear from their eyes, and
there will be no more death or sorrow
or crying or pain.
All these things are gone forever.

Revelation 21:4 NLT

It is said that one of the most unsafe places for a child molester is in prison. Though documentation is scant, the general notion is that prison populations form vigilante groups against those who have victimized innocent children.

This we know: child abusers are particularly vile, and according to the Scriptures, their day of judgment is coming.

It was heartrending to read the following letter from a woman who had been victimized as a child. Yet in her darkest times, Emmett Kelly, a famed clown with the Ringling Bros. and Barnum & Bailey Circus, brought her peace. Like Kelly's endearing character, Weary Willie, she was unable to smile.

A Smile from the Sad Clown

Weary Willie, the sad-faced clown, had a profound impact on my life as a child. I've always wanted to tell him that and thank him, but I never knew where to address my letter.

I had an aunt and uncle in Youngstown, Ohio, who my parents sometimes sent me to stay with when I was a child. My uncle was a clown and thought he was doing something special by taking me to see the circus and going backstage to meet the clowns.

What he didn't know was that I hated clowns.

Clowns were people who laughed and made everyone else laugh. I wasn't a happy child, and didn't want anyone trying to make me laugh.

No one knew that the reason I was sad was because my father was molesting me. In those days, no one talked about incest. No one taught us kids not to let people touch our private parts. I just thought this was what dads did. But I didn't like it. And it made me sad.

One day, I can't remember where, I saw a picture of Weary Willie. I immediately felt a kinship with him. I thought, "That clown feels just like me. He's sad!" As a young child, I always wished I could meet him, make him feel better, maybe even make him smile.

Fast-forward to November 2006. I was sitting alone in a lobby at the Cleveland Clinic while my husband underwent some tests. We had just been told he might have only a year to live. I was numb. No other way to describe it.

On the table next to me was a *Guideposts* magazine. I didn't feel like reading, but I picked it up to take my mind off what was going on. Oddly, there was an article about Emmett Kelly and the day Weary Willie, the sad-faced clown, was caught smiling in a session with a photographer. I had never heard that story. I continued reading.

Now this is where the godwinks became what I call a tender mercy for me. I read how Emmett had been interrupted by a phone call from a doctor telling him about the birth of his new baby daughter—Stasia! The photographer had snapped the picture, capturing Weary Willie smiling for the first and only time.

From the other side of the veil, I felt it was a strange communication, through my secret childhood friend Weary Willie, telling me it was okay for me to smile too—that everything would be fine and never to forget that the only person who made the sad-faced clown smile was Stasia.

You see, I know I'm not his daughter, but my name is Stasia too!

You're probably thinking, "How many people are named Stasia?" That's what I thought too. I'd never known anyone else with that name.

Perhaps you can imagine me sitting alone in that waiting room, burdened by the sad news about my husband, and how, for a little moment, I felt comfort.

Then God winked again. It turned out the doctors had made a mistake on my husband's medical analysis. His cancer had not spread! He had two different types of cancers, but both were treatable, and, thank God, he is still here with me!

I am glad I could finally tell this story, particularly so Emmett Kelly's daughter Stasia might hear of it. I only wish Weary Willie could have. I am sure he now has a permanent smile on his face. I hope this godwink letter will help someone else smile too.

Stasia Billiard

Our hearts break when we hear stories about little children whose innocence has been stolen from them by the heinous crime of molestation. How much more repulsive it is to learn it was a child's own father who committed the crime. The very person who should have been protecting the child is hurting the child. As Stasia attests, these young victims will carry emotional scars for years, if not for the rest of their lives.

We don't know why God permits evil—this will remain a mystery until we meet our Creator face-to-face. But we do know that the violator of a child will have hell to pay.

Whoever shall offend one of these little ones
who believe in me, it were better for him

*that a millstone were hanged about his
    neck,
and that he were drowned in the depth of
    the sea.*

Matthew 18:6 KJ2000

It's understandable how the abuse Stasia was forced to endure as a little girl translated to an unhappiness so deep that a smiling clown—the personification of happiness—would repel her, yet she would be drawn to a clown who appeared as sad as she was.

How we wish we could have counseled Stasia, years ago, that if you are in the midst of a crisis and feel you have nowhere to turn, cry out to Jesus. He is your protector and will give you strength in times of trouble.

*I have told you these things,
so that in me you may have peace.
In this world you will have trouble.
But take heart! I have overcome the world.*

John 16:33 NIV

14

What Should I Say When a Child Asks About Death?

Weeping may endure for a night,
but joy comes in the morning.

Psalm 30:5 NIV

When a child asks about death, the thoughts of even the most confident parent's brain may go into mine-sweeper mode searching for an appropriate thing to say.

Avoiding the question is not a good option. Children need to process the experience of loss just like the rest of us. On the other hand, telling them too much can overwhelm them. Striking a balance between those two points is the goal.

Most children have not been completely isolated from

the idea of death. Most have heard about it on television news programs or in movies; some have mourned the death of a pet.

The following godwink story from Kelly Morris Metzer exemplifies how death can come into a home when least expected.

A Brownie for Brownie

It was about four thirty in the afternoon when my younger son rushed up to me at the computer with a box of brownie mix in his hand, begging me to make brownies.

"I just need some brownies right now," he said.

I was in the middle of fixing a problem, and his dad was in the kitchen. "If Dad supervises, that will be okay."

And so he made the brownies.

About two hours later, I got a phone call from the brother-in-law of my close friend Michelle. He had shocking news. Michelle, whom I'd known for twenty-eight years, had died suddenly at 4:30 that afternoon. A mom of an eleven-year-old daughter, she had a special connection with my two boys, ages eleven and nine, so we all were devastated.

Then it dawned on me. Michelle had died at exactly the same time my son wanted to make brownies.

Sobbing, my son said, "I never want to eat brownies ever again."

You see, everyone knew Michelle by her nickname: Brownie.

I hugged my boys and reminded them that Brownie loved them. And us. I told them we would indeed have brownies again, and the treat would be even more special from now on.[1]

Kelly Morris Metzer

It appears that Kelly and her husband did exactly the right thing. They honestly talked with their sons about the sudden death of their friend and provided the boys with appropriate reassurances.

In talking with children about death, Hospice Net advises that we take the child's age into consideration.[2] They note that youngsters between the ages of five and nine realize that death is final; from age nine through adolescence, they begin to understand that it is irreversible; and in their teenage years, they may seek the meaning of life.

It's important to be honest with your children and not to delay informing them of a death. It can also be helpful for your children to see you grieve.[3]

Above all, let your child know that even in death, God is with us:

> *Never will I leave you;*
> *never will I forsake you.*
>
> Hebrews 13:5 NIV

For anyone who has lost a loved one, the feeling of sadness can be overwhelming. The old saying "Time heals all wounds" is difficult to wrap our minds around when we're experiencing fresh grief.

Dealing with loss is a personal experience. There is no time limit on the grieving process. You can't force it. It unfolds in its own time. There may be days when you feel like you are on an emotional roller coaster. Other times you may feel numb. You might cry until you wonder how a body could produce that many tears. Whatever you're experiencing, you need to allow the process to evolve.

I wonder if you know this: even Jesus cried. He experienced tremendous grief over his friend Lazarus, who had become sick and died. When Jesus arrived at the family's home, he found Lazarus' sisters, Mary and Martha, sobbing. He felt great compassion for them. He then went to the tomb of his friend and was swept away with grief. In the shortest verse of the Bible, we see the depth of pain even the Son of God felt as He mourned:

Jesus wept.

John 11:35 NIV

Jesus understands our grief. And he promised us:

I will not leave you comfortless:
I will come to you.

John 14:18 KJV

15

How Does God Reach Out to Connect with Me?

Don't forget to show hospitality to strangers,
for some who have done this
have entertained angels without realizing it!
Hebrews 13:2 NLT

We use the word *angel* pretty loosely in our everyday language. "You're an angel" is an endearment spoken by a mother to her children or a husband to his wife. There's the Los Angeles Angels baseball team of Anaheim; and we're pretty familiar with the once top-rated TV series *Touched by an Angel*. Then, somewhere in our memories is the image of a chubby cherub with a bow and arrow.

It makes you wonder if all these everyday references to

angels renders them merely symbolic. Surely they're not real.

Or are they?

It may surprise you that the word *angel* is mentioned 273 times in the Bible: 108 times in the Old Testament and 165 times in the New Testament. This is pretty direct evidence that God considers angels important.

Perhaps we would do well to reevaluate our attitudes about angels. After all, if angels are held in such high regard in God's book, the Bible, do we have reason to doubt the significant role angels may play our own lives? The word *angel* is a derivative of the Greek *aggelos*, which means "messenger." Might they indeed be messengers of goodness?

I receive quite a few letters from fans suggesting they've had a contemporary encounter with an angel. Laura's note is just one of them.

The Hug from Behind

When my father was dying of cancer, I struggled to keep up my strength. I was the youngest sibling, so I'd had my dad's attention more exclusively than the rest. I tried desperately to be there for my mom and the rest of my family, who were so distraught. But truth be known, I was dying inside.

One day I was visiting my husband's parents in their home, and my mother-in-law asked how my father was. Well, that was all it took. I had to excuse myself and leave to go cry in another room.

There I was, sobbing and just feeling so sorrowful, when I felt arms wrap around me. I leaned back in the warmth and kindness of that embrace, feeling so peaceful and loved and thankful my husband was there, knowing what I needed.

Minutes later, my husband walked in—through a doorway in front of me.

I turned around. There was no one behind me! Could it have been an angel?

I will forever be grateful for the peace I felt at that time. It was such a godwink![1]

Laura

As quoted at the start of this chapter, the Bible tells us that we may "have entertained angels without realizing it!" (Hebrews 13:2 NLT). Do you think that's what Laura experienced in her moment of deep anguish regarding her father? Could that hug have been a supernatural experience for her, comforting her with an angelic presence, wrapping her in love and providing peace when she needed it most?

I have had the privilege of interviewing several people who have had near-death experiences—some clinically dead for a considerable period of time—and they almost always report seeing multitudes of angels singing and praising God.

Angels, we can conclude, have a job to do. God has given them special assignments on our behalf. So today, feel confident that you may be "entertaining angels un-awares"—that angels may visit you as personal messengers from God, watching your back.

God may give you an angelic hug today too.

> *I am leaving you at peace.*
> *I am giving you my own peace.*
> *I am not giving it to you as the world gives.*
> *So don't let your hearts be troubled,*
> *and don't be afraid.*
>
> John 14:27 ISV

16

Some Days You Want to Throw in the Towel

If any of you lacks wisdom, he should ask God, who gives generously to all.

James 1:5 NIV

Are you going through a trial today?

Believe it or not, your solution may be as simple as making a request—asking God in prayer to help you. And when you ask, make sure you expect him to answer.

> *You do not have because you do not ask God.*
> James 4:2 NIV

Compare your situation to Alice's. She was feeling terrible insecurity. She had to make difficult health choices—

decisions she would have loved to run away from but couldn't. She was in a funk. Perhaps you've felt the same way.

On Quitting

Weighing postmastectomy treatment options for my best chance of living a healthy and long life after breast cancer, I was overwhelmed with the burden of decision making and worry.

After meeting with the oncologist, I sat at my kitchen table trying to settle my mind and review my options. I couldn't think straight, so I decided a cup of tea would make me feel better. I poured the tea and went to the refrigerator: no milk. I wasn't happy.

Since I had been crying for a good part of the day, I looked a mess. "I can't go to a supermarket like this," I thought. Instead, I decided to go to a drive-through dairy. As I drove, I thought about how surreal it was that the doctor was talking about *me* and *my life*.

Waiting in line at the dairy window, my mind drifted. My eyes settled on the white car in front of me, and there was my godwink: the license plate read, "DONT QUIT."

That divine message was just what I needed to do absolutely everything in my power to complete the recommended treatment.

I always wondered whatever happened to that car. Where did the driver live? If it was from my neighborhood, why had I never seen it before that evening?

A few weeks ago, I went to visit a friend. I stopped at a little store that I don't frequent much, and to my amazement, there it was again—the white car with the DONT QUIT license plate! I waited for the owner, told him my story, and personally thanked him for having everything to do with saving my life.

I am now a two-year breast cancer survivor (hooray!). I feel so blessed to have closure and my health![1]

Alice

Whatever issue you're wrestling with or insecurities you're feeling, take a clue from Alice. Put yourself in motion; step out in faith and *do* something about what's bothering you. Make a call. Get on the Internet. Go to the library. Find out more information. Ask a friend for advice. By stepping out in faith—believing that God is going to divinely align you with the people and information you need—you will uncover godwinks of comfort and confirmation.

Alice put herself in motion by going to the store, and along the way, she received the message of encouragement she needed: "DONT QUIT."

I wonder . . . what godwink awaits you?

Everything that was written in the past
was written to teach us,
so that through the endurance

*taught in the Scriptures
and the encouragement they provide
we might have hope.*

Romans 15:4 NIV

17

Can Anything Save My Child?

Let the little children come to me.

Luke 18:16

Gazing into the eyes of a doctor, frantically searching for answers that are not there, desperately attempting to process the horrible news he has just given you, is a parent's deepest moment of despair.

When Jada was told that her newborn child would likely die and that she should plan accordingly, she had two choices: collapse or fight. She chose the latter.

A mother of five and a successful motivational speaker and corporate coach, Jada Daves and her family put on the full armor of God and went into battle. Here's her story.

Baby Shafer

I am writing on behalf of my two-year-old son, Shafer. About a year and a half ago, Shafer was having a meltdown before nap-time. We had tried everything to calm him . . . singing, reading, rocking, playing DVDs . . . but nothing worked.

With his being so sick and fragile, I prayed for God to provide something to help soothe him. Then we "accidently" found Bill Gaither and his musical group on TV. From the minute Shafer heard the beautiful gospel music, he was mesmerized.

"More . . . more Gaifer," he would say. From then on, we have tuned in almost every day.

To give you a better understanding of our story, let me summarize. When Shafer was three weeks old, our doctor advised us to place our infant in hospice care and "just keep him comfortable."

The mother in me screamed, "NO!"

We proceeded to switch medical teams to assist our dying baby. The prognosis was grim as Shafer encountered one life-threatening issue after another. He was finally diagnosed with Denys-Drash syndrome, a medical condition so rare that only two hundred cases in the world have been documented.

At Vanderbilt Children's Hospital, he endured nine months of dialysis for eleven hours a day, and a feeding tube. Shafer continued to fight, but his kidneys eventually failed. We got the kidneys out just in time—missing full-blown cancer by weeks—so we skipped chemo and headed toward a transplant.

Then godwinks galore and another miracle occurred. As his mother, I was the perfect match to be Shafer's living donor. I cannot tell you how rare that is! The odds are one in multimillions that I would be a perfect match in six categories. Our story became not just one of miracles and faith but of a medical marvel inviting headlines: "Mother Gives Life to Son Twice!" Vanderbilt's own annual medical report was headlined, "Days of Miracle and Wonder."

More godwinks: Shafer's transplant surgeon was Dr. Shaffer, another physician was Dr. Schaeffer, and the ambulance transporting our son to Vanderbilt was flanked by Shaffer trucks on both sides. Is this all a mere coincidence? I think not!

Another godwink became clear as we recalled a Gaither program we had watched one night with tears and heavy hearts as TaRanda and Tony Greene shared their story of kidney failure. We were not quite sure why God had allowed us to see and hear their story at "such a time as this." But it all made sense months later when, as we awaited the transplant, my mom gave me a DVD as a gift. It featured Shafer's favorite song, "Thanks," but the video also "just happened" to have Tony and TaRanda's testimony on it.

God was assuring us that he knew right where we were and that we could trust him to be faithful, regardless of the final outcome.

We made it through the transplant and experienced miraculous success. Six months later, we are still listening to

the Gaithers' beautiful music every day as it lulls Shafer to
sleep. And our hearts are overflowing with gratitude.

Jada Daves

If you've ever heard Bill and Gloria Gaither's music
fests, like the one captured on a video titled *Giving Thanks*,
you know how they lift your spirits and soothe your soul.
Their musical gatherings are powerful affirmations of
God's love for us. Nearly every song is a prayer, especially
"Thanks" by Marshall Hall.

Still, it must have been difficult for Jada and her husband, Kevin, not to grow weary when their faith was tested.
They didn't know, from one week to the next, if Shafer
would live or die. They could only hope and pray that God
would save their baby's life.

But God knew, just as He knows the outcome for each
of us. God is never surprised by the circumstances we encounter; He knew about them long before we were born.

> *I knew you before I formed you
> in your mother's womb.*
> Jeremiah 1:5 NLT

Jada and Kevin trusted God even when all the odds
were stacked against them, when the doctor said there was
only a sliver of a chance that Jada's kidney would be a perfect match for her baby. And trusting God worked. God

85

winked. Jada miraculously met the criteria to donate her kidney to her precious child.

It's never easy to suffer through painful trials, especially when it involves our children, but we must never give up. As Jada said, God "knew right where we were . . . we could trust Him to be faithful, regardless of the final outcome."

> *Be strong and courageous. Do not be*
> *   afraid . . .*
> *for the* LORD *your God goes with you;*
> *he will never leave you nor forsake you.*
> Deuteronomy 31:6 NIV

And now Jada and her family are doing exactly what the Marshall Hall song says: giving thanks.

> *Thanks thanks I give you thanks for all*
> *   you've done*
> *. . . Oh Lord I give you thanks*[1]

18

What If I'm Not Ready to Be a Mother?

I have come that they may have life,
and have it to the full.

John 10:10 NIV

Kim was a mother-to-be facing a choice. She wrote this poignant letter expressing how God communicated to her through what she believed to be a godwink.

My Present from God

I was twenty years old and pregnant. I didn't want to have a baby. I'd never babysat for extra cash, and I'd never changed a diaper.

I knew the father of my child wouldn't be there for me, just like his father was never there for him. I also knew that my parents wouldn't talk to me because of my irresponsible behavior in getting pregnant.

I was terrified. I didn't know what to do.

I was afraid of having a baby, but I was also afraid for my soul. I went to my pastor and sought his advice. He said, "I can't tell you what to do. The best thing for you to do is to pray about it. Tell God you're desperate. Talk to him the same way you are speaking to me, and ask for an unmistakable sign."

So I laid out a strategy: to go ahead and *plan* to have an abortion but allow God to stop me if it wasn't the right choice.

I called the local Planned Parenthood and scheduled a pregnancy test. They had me fill out lots of paperwork and take a urine test. Someone gave me a piece of paper verifying that I was pregnant. I was told I would need that document for my next appointment and warned that if I didn't have it with me, they couldn't provide services. Then I spoke with a counselor for at least thirty minutes. She explained that Planned Parenthood wanted to make sure I wouldn't regret my decision and told me about the options of adoption and, if I decided to keep the baby, support services for single mothers. All in all, I spent an hour in their offices and finally made my decision to schedule an abortion. I had two weeks to wait.

That night I prayed and spoke candidly with God. I told him my fears about being a single mom without family support; my concerns about having a baby who would grow up without a dad; and my fear for my soul if I went ahead with the abortion. I also asked God what he would think of me if I did abort the baby.

Finally, I asked God for a clear sign, explaining, "I am scared. If your sign is too small, I will mistake it for coincidence, so please, God, make it a very obvious sign."

Two weeks went by. No sign.

I went for the scheduled appointment.

The trouble was, I couldn't find that document—the pregnancy slip. I knew I needed it. And my negligence in losing a piece of paper certainly didn't qualify as a sign from heaven. I went back to the Planned Parenthood office to see if I could get another copy. When I got there, the woman who had been so kind to me two weeks earlier didn't recognize me at all. They also had no record of my pregnancy test. The counselor I had spent a half hour with didn't recognize me or have a record of our conversation either. It was as if I had never been there.

I couldn't believe it. I was so stunned, I just left.

All the way home I thought, "How can they not remember me—and have no records?"

Then I realized: I did receive the answer to my prayer, after all. And that lost piece of paper was indeed a sign. Yes, I was terrified, but I committed myself to have the baby and to raise this child in faith. She would be God's daughter. He would be her Father.

Well, I had a beautiful baby girl, and I had so much fun raising her. Her name is Makayla.

It turned out that my family *was* there for me and helped raise her with enough love and support to turn out a lovely young woman.

From the time she was in kindergarten, Makayla has wanted to be a teacher, and today she is a college student pursuing her dream.

I did eventually find that "mysteriously lost" pregnancy slip. I laughed, and then I put it in her baby book. Makayla knows she's my gift from God and that she was born in faith—God's wink for me. For Christmas she gave me your book and wrote a note saying how it reminded her of our own story and how it was God's wink for both of us.

Kim McCormick

As a young woman, Kim had a choice. Because of the decision she made, she and Makayla have a life blessed with a wonderful mother-daughter relationship.

In the Bible we are told:

> *My people are destroyed*
> *from lack of knowledge.*

Hosea 4:6 NIV

It's one thing to know your Bible, but it's another thing to know the God of the Bible. Many people are robbed of blessings that rightfully belong to them because they don't know God's promises.

Yet how often do even we, who know his promises, listen to what society tells us to the exclusion of what God's Word has to tell us.

> *You will know the truth,*
> *and the truth will set you free.*
>
> John 8:32 NIV

If you are considering an abortion, please know that no matter how dire your situation, God will work something beautiful in your life if you trust Him and have faith in His Word.

If you have already had an abortion, your choices of the past cannot be erased—but if you ask for God's forgiveness, He will help you to heal so you can move forward.

19

How Can I Hear the Voice of God?

Does the one who makes the human ear not hear?
Does the one who forms the human eye not see?
Psalm 94:9 NET

Have you ever had a thought in your head that seemed to speak loud and clear?

Before you say, "No, I don't hear voices inside my head," let me ask this: Have you ever replayed the voice of a singer in your head? I mean, right now, could you imagine the voice of Tony Bennett singing "I Left My Heart in San Francisco"? Or the Beatles singing, "She loves you, yeah, yeah, yeah"? Could you conjure up in your head the voice of Whitney Houston singing her classic rendition of the national anthem?

So . . . if you can hear a *song* in your head . . . you should be able to hear a *voice* speaking to you, right?

What, then, would you do if a distinct, authoritative voice inside your head suddenly gave you a specific, forceful command? This letter from Dean Beyer suggests it would be a good idea to pay attention. It might be God trying to save your life.

The Voice

Our church volunteered to help a woman who was moving from Arizona to Las Vegas. We finished loading all of her belongings into a U-Haul truck, and my wife, Sue, and I started the drive to Nevada.

After arriving and unloading, Sue and I had dinner in Vegas, then headed back home around six thirty that evening. It was dark by the time we arrived at the Hoover Dam. We found ourselves behind an eighteen wheeler on the two-lane road, so I patiently stayed behind the truck. I knew the road would remain two lanes for ten miles, then expand to three lanes for the next two miles.

At the ten-mile marker, I pulled out into the middle lane and began passing the semi. As we went past the cab of the truck, I heard a voice.

"Pull over in front of the truck."

I glanced down, confirming that the car radio was off. Sue had fallen asleep, so she wasn't speaking to me. I had no idea where the voice could have come from.

I looked into my rearview mirrors to check for any traffic in the lane behind me. There was none. So, I reasonably concluded, there was no reason to pull in front of the truck immediately. Besides, the lane I was in wouldn't end for about a mile, so I had plenty of time.

But the voice came back—this time loud and stern, ordering: "PULL OVER IN FRONT OF THE TRUCK NOW!"

I had served in the military for twenty-one years, so my response was an immediate, "Yes, sir." I pulled over, in front of the truck, as commanded.

Just as I came into the right lane, I nearly collided with a large object that was in the lane I had just left! It wasn't moving, and I missed it by less than a foot.

I looked quickly in my side mirror and saw the object illuminated by the headlights of the truck behind me and another car going by in the opposite direction. It was a full-grown burro standing in the middle lane!

Had I hit that burro at sixty-five miles per hour, I'm certain Sue and I would have been killed.

"Did you see that?" I shouted to Sue, waking her up.

"No," she replied blinking her eyes sleepily.

"Did you hear a voice?"

She looked at me. "No."

I had not been praying at the time, but I know what I heard, and it had to be a voice from above that saved our lives. I will never forget it.

Dean H. Beyer

In a separate note, Sue writes:

We believe God winked at that moment, allowing us to continue living. I never heard the voice, but Dean did. That's what counts. We thank God and never will forget that godwink. Dean, especially, is on the lookout for the "still small voice" and awaiting his next command.

Sue Beyer

One of our favorite preachers, seen worldwide on Sunday mornings, is Dr. Charles Stanley. Often, in his sermons, he says, "Listen." When he says that, he is signaling that he's about to make an important point.

Sometimes God does that with us. He says, "Listen." It might be through a quickening in our spirit or, in the case of Dean Beyer, through a distinct voice inside our head.

Don't tune God out.

The Bible tells us God spoke to the prophet Elijah in a "still small voice" (1 Kings 19:12 KJV). What is that "still small voice"? Perhaps it's the voice Dean heard. Or maybe the Lord will speak to you in another way.

How do you know it's God? Those who have heard his voice answer, with firmness, "You'll know!"

A mother can always recognize her own child's cry on a noisy playground. Might that be the same principle here? That when you hear God's voice, you won't question it— you'll know it?

Another verse of Scripture reinforces that premise:

> *Whether you turn to the right or to the left,*
> *your ears will hear a voice behind you,*
> > *saying,*
> *"This is the way; walk in it."*
>
> Isaiah 30:21 NIV

20

I Have So Little—How Can I Give?

*A poor widow came
and put in two small copper coins,
which amount to a cent.*

Mark 12:42 NASB

When we have little to spare—just enough money to get by, barely enough food for the week, nothing left for luxuries—it's difficult to think about giving it away.

It's easy to jealously guard what we have, and easy to justify it: "Hey, I worked hard for this, get your own!" Or perhaps, softer: "I know you have needs, but I'm in the same situation. I'm sorry, I just can't help you."

But as valid as they might seem, I wonder how those arguments would measure up against the hero in this story.

Rags and Winks

My best friend and I took a weekend trip to Baltimore. I was flat broke, but Christy said, "Don't worry about it—I don't have much money, but I'll pay for gas, food, and hotel."

We checked into the hotel, Christy paid with her credit card, and we headed out for a burger. While getting our food, she sat her purse on the counter and turned around to get some napkins.

When we sat down to eat, a panicked look came over Christy's face. She realized her wallet was missing from her purse. Frantic, we searched all around the restaurant, but the wallet was gone.

We now had no money, no credit cards, and no way back home, since the car gas gauge had been on empty when we parked it at the hotel. We walked down the street, searching for the wallet, and finally found it in a trash can. All the cash and credit cards were gone. We felt defeated, but we were grateful that at least Christy had gotten her ID back. We concluded that we had no choice but to leave the next morning.

The next day, we pulled past a dirty, homeless man and into a gas station, where we began rummaging through our purses for loose change in hopes of finding enough to get us home. We scoured the car. We looked under seat cushions and floor mats, cheering each time we found a quarter. Our mood actually turned jovial, and we kept assuring ourselves, "God will handle this. We'll be fine."

As we dug for more change, we noticed that the homeless man was watching us curiously. We smiled, waved hello, and went on about our business.

Several minutes later, the homeless man walked up to the car and asked what we were doing. Laughing and shaking our heads at the mess we were in, we quickly explained the situation.

"You girls shouldn't be in this part of town," said the man. He then handed us his paper cup full of change—the money he'd begged for all morning long. Over his shoulder, as he walked away, he hollered, "Get home safe."

We were astounded . . . and very grateful . . . that God had sent us this unlikely angel. Many other people, well dressed, with fancy cars, had come and gone that morning at the gas station, but none had offered to help. It was the man in rags who delivered God's love to us.

The money he gave us bought just enough gas to get us home. Safely.

Debbie

The homeless man in Debbie's letter reminds us of the poor widow Jesus spoke about.

> *Calling his disciples to him, Jesus said,*
>   *"Truly I tell you,*
> *this poor widow has put more into the*
>   *treasury than all the*

others. They all gave out of their wealth;
but she, out of her
poverty, put in everything—all she had to
live on."

Mark 12:43–44 NIV

It wasn't the folks with the fancy cars who helped Christy and Debbie. It was the homeless man with heart. He gave freely everything he had in his cup. He had compassion for Christy and Debbie.

Moreover, it wasn't the amount he gave but that he gave with a cheerfulness.

God loves a cheerful giver.

2 Corinthians 9:7 NIV

Even though we know the Bible tells us to be cheerful and generous givers, we can still find ourselves protesting, "But what if I don't have money to spare?"

Fact is, we can be generous with our time, our talents, or in any number of ways. I have a writer friend who says he "tithes" his contacts for up-and-coming writers. One of the poorest people in our church, Helen, is a ninety-year-old widow who never fails to bake a pie and send a homemade greeting card to someone who is hurting.

I'm confident that God will show you where you can meet a specific need for someone too. Inviting him over for dinner? Mentoring someone? Perhaps just letting a neighbor who is having a difficult time know that you will be praying for her at a specific time each day?

When we give to others, we are surely blessed too. That's one of God's promises.

> *He who sows sparingly and grudgingly will*
> *   also reap sparingly and*
> *grudgingly, and he who sows generously . . .*
> *   will also reap*
> *generously and with blessings.*
>
> 2 Corinthians 9:6

ENCOURAGEMENT

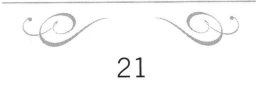

21

How Do I Face the Unknown?

Perfect love drives out fear.

1 John 4:18 NIV

Fear of the unknown is akin to something else we don't like: uncertainty.

When you lose your job or someone you love, it's easy to doubt your talents or whether anyone really cares about you. At times like these, drawing closer to God will help you balance your emotions and provide comfort and reassurance. It will help you to understand that He allows some uncertainty in life so you will go to Him and His Word for answers.

Sheri has a sweet story that helps to make this point.

The Christmas Cactus

When my firstborn started preschool in 1999, I had to buy him a plant for a school project. At the store, the only plant available was a Christmas cactus. My memories instantly took me back to summers spent at my grandmother's house, where several Christmas cacti sat on her windowsills. So I bought it.

As a military family, we moved from state to state and took that plant with us from Washington to Rhode Island, Virginia, California, and our present home in Pennsylvania.

Three years later, in 2002, the cactus finally bloomed for the first time—during my grandmother's stay with us over Christmas. I did not know at the time that it would be the last time she would stay with us. She later died from malignant melanoma.

Over the years, I have tried every trick in the book to get that cactus to bloom again. It just wouldn't. I've put it in dark, cold areas, starting in early October; I've gone without watering it; and I've tried various other techniques recommended for forcing a cactus to bloom. Nothing worked. One year I almost killed it accidentally by trying to force the blooms.

We subsequently moved 3,500 miles for my husband's job—with three special-needs kids and the cactus. This past February, my husband was suddenly laid off without warning. It was devastating to our entire family. We were fearful and struggled with uncertainty.

A short while later, I noticed the cactus had strange buds appearing on the tips. Day by day, they changed. Then I realized the cactus was trying to flower!

It was in full bloom on March 28—my grandmother's birthday.

That was the most amazing godwink. It was as if God were tapping on our shoulders to remind us of my grandmother . . . and that everything would be fine.

Sheri Mellott

Sheri "tried every trick in the book to get that cactus to bloom again." Still, it wouldn't. Not until God was ready for it to bloom, for His purposes, on His timetable.

God has a plan for you, to help you emerge from your place of uncertainty and fear about the unknown. It may not be revealed right away, and it isn't easy to wait on God. But His Word reassures us He knows what He's doing:

> *"My thoughts are not your thoughts,*
> *nor are your ways My ways," declares the*
> LORD.

Isaiah 55:8 NASB

Just as with the flowering of a Christmas cactus, it is in the waiting that God does His best work. Your life can flower just like Sheri's little cactus.

Go ahead. Reach up and grasp God's hand, and He will direct you, reduce your fear of uncertainty, and—in His perfect timing—help you to bloom where you're planted.

For you did not receive a spirit
that makes you a slave again to fear,
but you received the Spirit of sonship.
And by him we cry, "Abba, Father."

Romans 8:15 NIV

22

What Can I Do That Pleases God the Most?

You shall love your neighbor as yourself.

Mark 12:31 ESV

The concept of neighbors helping neighbors has been with us forever.

We often see it most prominently when there's a tragedy or natural disaster. After tornados and hurricanes, a powerful force springs up in a community: neighbors helping each other, often under the leadership of churches and civic organizations. It unfolds almost instantly, long before national agencies like FEMA or the Red Cross are able to get on the scene.

In most small towns across the country, when a family experiences the loss of a loved one, a neighbor will soon be knocking on the door with a covered dish or a pie.

The act of generosity is in our makeup, and we are taught from childhood that good deeds please God. Remember the Golden Rule:

> *In everything, do to others*
> *what you would have them do to you.*
> Matthew 7:12 NIV

Wesley's letter is all about being a good neighbor.

State Farm Man

I wasn't in town when my dad had a fatal heart attack while mowing the lawn. Everything I heard came secondhand, and I never met or was able to thank the person who tried to save Dad's life.

My dad was a State Farm insurance agent for nearly forty years in Aurora, Missouri, which is about forty-five miles from Joplin. I worked with him for seventeen years prior to his retirement.

After the devastating Joplin tornado of May 22, 2011, like so many other folks, I was in a holding pattern waiting to get my insurance claim processed. I walked in to a Joplin State Farm office swamped with ringing phones and waiting customers. From force of habit, without thinking, I sat down at an empty work station and asked, "Who's next?"

A young woman had lost her home and everything she owned.

She had been to the local bank and was trying to stop her monthly mortgage obligation on a home that had been destroyed. So I called the bank to see if I could help. While the bank kept me on hold, I made small talk about the storm. Looking at her papers, I noted that her temporary address was near my mom's. We discovered that her parents lived only one house away.

Surprised, I said I'd heard that after my dad had his heart attack, her parents had brought a casserole to my mom, just to be neighborly.

With tears in her eyes, the young woman recounted that she had been visiting her parents the day of my dad's heart attack and, when the fire truck arrived, she had run over to my parents' house to see if she could help. She is a registered nurse, and she had performed CPR until the ambulance got there.

What a gift—a godwink—out of the tragedy of the storm, to meet her and finally say thank you for trying to save Dad's life.

Wesley

State Farm Insurance has one of the most familiar advertising slogans. Perhaps you can even sing the jingle that's been around for years: "Like a good neighbor, State Farm is there." You could say that State Farm is right in sync with the Bible:

> *You shall love your neighbor as yourself.*
> James 2:8 NKJV

With God, it's not a marketing philosophy but the way we should live our lives every day.

The registered nurse who ran to a neighbor's house and started CPR on a man who turned out to be Wesley's dad was demonstrating God's commandment to "Love your neighbor as yourself."

Did you know the Bible tells us eight times to love our neighbors? Loving our neighbors is part of God's plan to demonstrate His love to His people.

> *Instruct them to do as many good deeds*
> *as they can and to help everyone.*
>
> 1 Timothy 6:18 CEV

Imagine if this concept of neighbors helping neighbors were the basis for a Web site helping neighbors to connect needs with acts of kindness in cities and towns across the land . . . what amazing things could happen!

We have helped to launch just such a movement: it's called networkofneighbors.com.

> *My children, our love*
> *should not be just words and talk;*
> *it must be true love,*
> *which shows itself in action.*
>
> 1 John 3:18 GNT

23

What Can I Do When I Feel Discouraged?

My tears have been my food day and night,
while people say to me all day long,
"Where is your God?"

Psalm 42:3 NIV

Have you ever said or thought, "Where are you, God? Are you listening to me?"

It should come as little surprise, then, to realize that the psalmist David also expressed that sentiment.

We go through our daily lives, sometimes like a Ping-Pong ball bouncing off the obstacles we encounter, tested by stress-inducing issues and people. Have you ever felt like you just wanted to pull up the covers and hide from the world?

Sometimes, when you are at your most vulnerable, a nonbelieving observer might kick you while you are down, taunting, "Where's your God now, huh? If He's so big, watching over you, why isn't He coming to your rescue?"

Perhaps the enemy, who loves everything "dis"—*dis*cord, *dis*couragement, and *dis*illusion—has just gotten his foot into the door of your mind.

Look what happened with Dan Appel:

When Spirits Are Low

As a pastor of a church in Northern California, I've learned that churchgoers are not always the most gracious people in the world, especially with their pastors. It's easy for them to forget that we are just as human as they are.

After eight years of struggling under difficult and painful circumstances to help my church family become what God knows they could be, I was at the end of my emotional and spiritual rope. I had had one of those horrific weeks that make you want to quit the ministry and take up plumbing. It was topped off by a church member who looked me in the eye and said, "Pastor, I think you're the worst preacher in the world." Then, after a committee meeting at the church, I heard one of my leaders say to another as they left the room, "We need to get a new pastor."

I have no illusions. I know I was sent to this church by my denomination because it was a church with a history of emotional and spiritual violence toward their pastors. But the remarks by those two people took all of the wind out of my sails.

For two days I staggered around, praying, "God, you led Israel out of Egypt; can't you please free me to leave this place? If there is any value in my life and ministry, you are going to have to show me, because I cannot go any further."

Later, as I drove up to the church, a man motioned for me to stop. It was the regent of a local college who had been attending our church for six months. He walked over to the car and said, "Dan, I just want to thank you for your ministry to me and my family and our church. Your sermons are a real blessing, and I really appreciate the vision God has given you for our church."

I asked him to wait while I parked my car. As we walked to the church, I thanked him for allowing God to "wink" at me through him that day.

Puzzled, he asked, "What do you mean?"

I shared how a book I had just read (*When God Winks at You*) had sensitized me to the way God constantly reaches out to affirm and strengthen us through seemingly coincidental events.

Since that day, whenever we cross paths, the regent winks at me and says, "Dan, how's it going?"

As a postscript, I bought the book and gave it to him. He smiled as he looked at it and said, "I am really going through some tough times this week. I needed a wink from God. Thanks."

Dan M. Appel

Pastors don't just preach on Sunday and take the rest of the week off. They wear many hats. In our small church, our pastor is the administrator, youth minister, children's minister, family therapist . . . the list goes on and on. And while juggling all those roles, he also has to get ready for next Sunday morning.

Ministers can look to the ancient Scriptures to give them sustenance:

> *They that wait upon the LORD*
> *shall renew their strength;*
> *they shall mount up with wings as eagles;*
> *they shall run, and not be weary;*
> *and they shall walk, and not faint.*
>
> Isaiah 40:31 KJV

Dan sure didn't feel like an eagle when someone said, to his face, "You are the worst preacher in the world." He was disheartened. And when he overheard others talking about replacing him, his confidence was shaken. All he wanted to do was disappear. But, instead, he came against the enemy with prayer.

The devil uses discouragement as one of his strongest weapons. Therefore, every day, we need to remind ourselves to put on the full armor of God.

> *Put on the full armor of God, so that you*
> *can*

take your stand against the devil's schemes.
For our struggle is not against flesh and
  blood, but . . .
against the powers of this dark world . . .
Therefore put on the full armor of God, so
  that
when the day of evil comes,
you may be able to stand your ground.
                    Ephesians 6:11–13 NIV

Remember, God designed you to fly like an eagle. So you mustn't allow harsh words to throw you into a tailspin.

As for our pastors, let's keep them under a canopy of prayer. The enemy attacks them nonstop just because they are servants of God. Right now, let's lift up our pastors in prayer, asking God, the great encourager, to give them strength to carry on.

24

I'm Concerned About the Influence of Hollywood on My Kids

When someone has been given much,
much will be required in return;
and when someone has been entrusted with much,
even more will be required.

Luke 12:48 NLT

Do celebrities, television, and movies negatively influence the behavior of our children? A survey of parents suggests they do. "Two-thirds say they are very concerned about the amount of inappropriate media content children in this country are exposed to, and many believe media is a major contributor to young people's violent or sexual behaviors."[1]

How many of us have lamented, "Oh, if we only could return to the golden age of television—there were only three channels, but more to watch! And everything was clean!"

As a television network executive for several decades, I wonder how many current TV shows will have the lasting values of some of those great series of the past: *The Andy Griffith Show, I Love Lucy, Leave It to Beaver,* and *The Carol Burnett Show.* These were programs that promoted good family values and significantly influenced millions of children in a positive manner.

My wonderful wife, Louise, like many of us, was glued to the TV every Saturday night for *The Carol Burnett Show.* She was not only influenced by Carol but grew up to be a comedic impressionist who can look and sound just like her.

Here's a sweet note from Paula Gervais, who caught Louise on a morning talk show.

A Carol Burnett Connection

SQuire, please tell your lovely wife, Louise, that I watched the clip on the *Today* show of her doing an impression of Carol Burnett and her story about how she met Carol. She was absolutely hysterical. Tell her we have something in common.

I, too, grew up idolizing Carol and her comedic abilities. When I was about fifteen or so, I wrote a fan letter and sent along an idea for a comedy sketch. Some time later, while watching her show one night, my family and I noticed that the skit she was doing was very similar to the one I had suggested. Soon after that, I received a delightful letter typed on an old-fashioned typewriter (there were no computers then) from Carol Burnett herself, with her signature.

But here was the godwink: the letter was written on the date of my birthday—April 28!

At the time, I thought, "Wow—what a coincidence." But now, as an adult, I know there are no coincidences . . . only godwinks."

Paula Gervais

Paula's godwink, realizing that Carol Burnett had written to her on her birthday, forged an even stronger connection between her and her heroine.

Our childhood heroes can help shape the path we will follow for the rest of our lives. Carol Burnett is someone who has affected thousands. She has exemplified wonderful qualities in her personal and professional life. She is always kind to others, has an incredible sense of humor, and has mentored many young people who wanted to have a career in theater and television.

It's sad to say, but the good role models for our children today are few and far between. You can pick up any newspaper and see the names of athletes who are involved in illegal activities, politicians abusing their power, celebrities engaging in unsavory behavior, and even ministers and priests who have been pulled into the enemy's clutches.

Positions of fame and prominence can be used for good or evil. One of the most famous recent heroes is football player Tim Tebow. Besides being known for his Heisman Trophy and winning two BCS National Football Championships, he is best known for his love of Jesus Christ and for unashamedly praying on the field. He exemplifies good character—humility, dedication, kindness, and loyalty—on and off the football field. His motto for the Tim Tebow Foundation is "Bringing faith, hope and love to those needing a brighter day in their darkest hour of need."

Tim tries to live his life according to *his* hero, the one he looks up to and bows down before; the only perfect role model. His name is Jesus.

> *. . . set an example for the believers in speech, in life, in love, in faith and in purity.*
>
> 1 Timothy 4:12

25

Does God Control My Life, or Do I?

*LORD, make me know my end
and what is the measure of my days.*

Psalm 39:4 ESV

Famed pastor Rick Warren wrote: "People ask me, what is the purpose of life?"

He responds this way: "In a nutshell, life is preparation for eternity. We were made to last forever, and God wants us to be with Him in heaven.

"One day my heart is going to stop, and that will be the end of my body—but not the end of me. I may live sixty to one hundred years on earth, but I am going to spend trillions of years in eternity. This is the warm-up act—the dress rehearsal.

"We were made *by* God and *for* God, and until you figure that out, life isn't going to make sense."[1]

Discovering that each new day on earth is a gift for which we need to be thankful is an awakening Shirlean experienced through a simple godwink.

The Lug Nuts

My husband, Bill, and I decided to move to Arizona to get away from the harsh winters of Pennsylvania. We had a large family: his three boys by a previous marriage, and our three girls.

We rented a U-Haul trailer, loaded it with our possessions, and hooked it up to our very old Dodge pickup.

We had been on the road for three days and made it to just outside of Santa Rosa, New Mexico, when I suddenly had such pain in my abdomen that I asked Bill to pull over at the next rest area. I went into the restroom, but the pains suddenly disappeared as quickly as they had come.

When I came back out to get into the truck, Bill was as white as a sheet. I asked him what was wrong. He took me to the driver's side and pointed to the rear wheel. I almost fainted. Three of the five lug nuts on that wheel had somehow broken off and only two nuts were still holding the tire on.

If we had lost that wheel, the truck would have flipped. It could have been a disaster, killing or severely injuring Bill, me, and all of our children.

I knew at that moment that someone was watching over us, very closely, and I will never ever forget how blessed we were that day. More than once I've thought about that mysterious yet temporary stomachache—a godwink—causing us to pull off the road.

Shirlean A. Hansen

Disasters happen quickly. Shirlean's story reminds us that life can be over in a blink of an eye. So often we take life for granted instead of acknowledging that the present is a present—a gift from God almighty.

> *God is our protection and our strength.*
> *He always helps in times of trouble.*
> Psalm 46:1 NCV

Think of it. If it weren't for the godwink of Shirlean's stomachache, the entire family could have been in a tragic accident.

> *Teach us to number our days,*
> *that we may gain a heart of wisdom.*
> Psalm 90:12 WEB

Only God knows the number of your days, but you can choose how you live them. When you get on the highway of life, God gives you the free will to go too fast, too slow, or just the right speed. You can choose to live recklessly or responsibly. You can choose to stay on the path or get off on the byways of life. Your choice. Your free will.

On the other hand, when you give your life over to God and allow Him to be your navigator, all your journeys will bring you to the proper destination.

26

My Pain and Grief Are Unbearable—How Can I Go On?

He is my loving God and my fortress,
my stronghold and my deliverer, my shield,
in whom I take refuge . . .

Psalm 144:2 NIV

In the Bible, more is said about eagles than any other bird. Eagles are mentioned twenty-six times, and God uses their majesty and strength to teach us many lessons. For instance, did you know that eagles do not fear nor fly from a storm? Instead, they allow powerful wind currents to lift them above all the turmoil.

God does that for you too.

When your life is turned upside down by tragedy or the

loss of a loved one, you can count on God to be the wind beneath your wings. Just call on Him.

Imagine being at John Campbell's side the day he dissolved into tears at the loss of his dear wife yet was lifted by the Spirit on the wings of eagles.

On Eagles' Wings

It is not easy to lose one's spouse—someone who had watched out for me for all our married lives, thirty-nine years. Marsha passed away early in the morning on May 27, 2008, as I was holding her hand and stroking her head.

Prior to her passing, we had discussed various matters, putting things in order, including what music she wanted played at her service.

"'On Eagles' Wings,'" she'd said.

As per her wish, it was done.

They say the two most stressful things one encounters are the loss of a loved one and moving. Well, both of those stressors occurred for me in the same week.

My three wonderful sisters came down to Florida from New England to help me sort through Marsha's things, pack our things from the rental house, and get ready for the move to the "new" house Marsha and I had purchased just before her health failed.

My nerves were stretched to the breaking point. As I picked up a box that I had just packed, it ripped, and all the contents tumbled onto the floor. My emotions got the better of me. I said a few things I shouldn't have and stormed out of the house.

I fled to the field next to the house to be alone, tears pouring from my eyes as apprehension rose in my heart.

"Marsha, honey, I need your help," I cried out. "I need to know you're okay . . . and that everything's going to be all right."

My mind went to the song, her song, "On Eagles' Wings."

"Honey, show me an eagle . . . I need to see an eagle," I said urgently.

At that moment, a voice in my head said, "Turn around." So I did.

Coming over the roof of the house were *two* eagles—a pair!

I called my sisters out to ask if they saw what I saw. They did. Two raptors circled overhead and then flew off.

Never again will I doubt the power of our Creator and the power of love.

I know now that Marsha is okay—that she is in heaven. Yet, in a way, she's still with me too. I feel her love and comfort. But I sure miss her hugs.

John Campbell

How our hearts broke for our dear friend John.

Few would wish to trade their loss for his. Yet your heart may be breaking today too. Do you wonder how you can possibly go on without that dear person in your life? Do you dread getting out of bed every day, knowing you're going to have to revisit tender memories that are also so painful?

No matter how deep your grief, rest assured that God

knows that, and that He is with you every step of the way. Lift up your hand, right now, and grasp His. It's there, outstretched to you.

Meet Him in His Word. Those passages, which have soothed so much heartache over so many centuries, are there to sustain you during your darkest time of grief. God will give you peace that surpasses all understanding. After all these years, these words—His message to you—are still relevant. Like the powerful eagle,

> *He will cover you with his feathers,*
> *and under his wings you will find refuge;*
> *his faithfulness will be your shield*
> *and rampart.*

Psalm 91:4 NIV

The lyrics to the song Marsha requested for her funeral were written by a priest, Jan Michael Joncas. "On Eagles' Wings" was subsequently recorded by such artists as Josh Groban and Michael Crawford. And how appropriate they are to our conversation:

> *And he will raise you up on eagles' wings,*
> *. . . and hold you in the palm of his hand.*[1]

We pray that a new day will dawn for you, raising you on the wings of eagles from darkness to a day of sunshine and joy, filled with God's winks.

27

Thank God for Grandmas!

Start children off in the way they should go,
and even when they are old they will not turn from it.
Proverbs 22:6 NIV

One wonders how many children are raised by their grandmothers. For whatever reason, at the time, it just wasn't possible for Mom to raise them, and Grandma jumped in to help out.

One in every three households is led by grandparents, according to a survey conducted by Grandparents.com, and 61 percent of grandparents take care of or babysit their grandkids on a regular basis.

Think how the world might have been cheated if a strong grandma had not stood as a moral compass in the lives of James Earl Jones, Jack Nicholson, or Carol Burnett.

Carol talks about her grandmother Nanny, as the central character of her formative years and the reason she always pulled her ear at the end of each episode of her show. Carol once relayed this conversation:

"Nanny, I'll pull my ear for you."

"Your what?"

"My ear. It'll be our special secret signal. From me to you. Telling you, 'I love you, Nanny.'"[1]

I thought about that when I saw this quote about grandmothers:

> *A grandmother is a special person*
> *who causes a joyful happening in the*
> *heart of a child.*[2]

Another grandmother was celebrated in this charming letter from Lois Ann:

Small Shirts, Small Winks

I have two younger brothers who are only a year apart in age. Fifty years ago, when my youngest brother was two years old, my parents divorced and my grandmother came to live with and care for us. She was a godly, loving grandma to three small, motherless children, and she was determined to raise us to know Jesus as our Savior.

Every Sunday, Grandma would dress the boys in identical

shirts and take us all to church. Many people thought the boys were twins.

Years passed, and my grandmother died. The boys grew up and apart from each other, moving to different states: Michigan and Arizona. Then, in 2006, we had a family reunion. My brothers had not seen each other in several years, nor had they spoken for some time. But everyone was blown away when they both showed up at the reunion wearing identical shirts—purchased in different states! No one could explain the "coincidence," or what you call a godwink, and everyone marveled at it.

It was a great opportunity to reminisce about how much our godly grandma had loved them, prayed every day for them, and had taken them to church every Sunday for many years . . . dressed just alike.

Lois Ann Vernier

Lois Ann's grandma, like many grandmothers, was the axis of faith in the family, making sure everyone toed the line, went to church, and was introduced to the wisdom of the Bible.

Perhaps you can recall a grandmother who frequently quoted the Bible. What would we do without them? Considerable evidence shows that when we teach our children biblical principles, they grow up to be more polite, honest, and civil human beings.

Children should know that, just as their grandmothers have taught them, the Bible provides the perfect guidelines for our lives. Jesus said:

*I did not come to abolish the law of
Moses . . .
I came to accomplish their purpose.*
Matthew 5:17 NLT

Taking action as parents and grandparents to teach our children to love God and to love their neighbors as themselves will indeed bring up a child in the ways of the Lord.

28

It's Just Too Hard to Say Goodbye

*We would rather be away from these earthly
bodies,
for then we will be at home with the Lord.*
2 Corinthians 5:8 NLT

No matter how much our rational mind tells us that losing
a loved one is a "natural process," it is still hard to grasp.
No matter how long we've known that we are going to lose
our parents, there still is never enough preparation. When
it happens, we find ourselves in a place heavy with heartache.

Jim Kelley was in that place. He writes that he couldn't
even bear to go to his mother's bedside to say goodbye.

Jimmy's Goodbye

My name is Jim. My mom always called me Jimmy. On December 31, my sweet mother passed away. We knew she was close to leaving us, and all her family had gathered at the nursing home.

The priest went into her room and anointed her. As he left, the electricity flickered off and then came back on. An hour later, the fire alarm went off. The nursing staff couldn't figure out why.

The hospice nurse told us it was time—that we should go into the room and say our final goodbyes. I couldn't go. It was too hard for me. I felt bad, but I just couldn't go see her in that state and have that as my final memory of my wonderful mother.

Moments later, I became aware that the nursing home music system had been playing music all along. Just then, a song came on that Mom used to sing to me when I was a boy. It was "Goodbye Jimmy, Goodbye." She passed away three minutes later.

I believe that God was giving my mother another way to say goodbye to me—through a sign from him that he was taking her to heaven—and letting me know it was okay.

These are the words:

> I'll see you again but I don't know when
> Goodbye, Jimmy, goodbye[1]

Jim

What a sweet sentiment, from God to Jim, at a time when he was hurting. Isn't it just like God to use a song that Jim's mother had sung to him in childhood to reassure him, just as a mother would do, that everything was going to be okay?

I suspect that God was also helping Jim to understand that it is a glorious day when a loved one graduates to his or her eternal home—even though we, here on earth, are left behind, feeling empty and focused on the horrible thought of never seeing our loved one again. We desperately want one last hug, one last kiss, one last good-bye.

God knows our sadness. He wants to comfort us—and, at the same time, to let us know that we can take joy and solace in the promise of heaven. He wants us to know that even the most beautiful, perfect day here on earth could never compare with what is awaiting our loved ones and us in heaven. Remember the Bible's stunning description:

> *The wall was made of jasper, and the city of pure gold, as pure as glass. The foundations of the city walls were decorated with every kind of precious stone. The first foundation was jasper, the second sapphire, the third agate, the fourth emerald, the fifth onyx, the sixth ruby, the seventh chrysolite, the eighth beryl, the ninth topaz, the tenth turquoise, the eleventh jacinth, and the twelfth amethyst. The twelve gates were twelve*

pearls, each gate made of a single pearl.
The great street of the city was of gold, as
pure as transparent glass.
Revelation 21:18–21 NIV

The perfect song coming over the hospital sound system at precisely the right moment was a godwink. It was God's way of saying to Jim that his mom was more than all right; she was now in that beautiful place, standing at her Savior's side.

PRAYER
ENCOURAGEMENT

29

What Can I Do When I've Lost Something Valuable?

Do not worry about anything, but
pray and ask God for everything you need,
always giving thanks.

Philippians 4:6 NCV

It's a terrible feeling.

You had your wallet a short while ago, but now it's gone. You can't imagine where it could be. You frantically search and search. Your mind races to form a clear memory of when you last held it; where you were standing.

And when you conclude that it is nowhere to be found, you calculate the trouble you're in—what you will do without that money, or what hassles you will go through if your identity is stolen by the person who finds your license and credit cards. You feel violated and slump into a posture of helplessness.

Here's a story about a woman who felt that way. But, like each of us, God was watching out for her. In her case, he used a godwink and a police officer named Jeff Harvey to help her.

Just a Routine Godwink, Ma'am

While working as a deputy in Cincinnati, I pulled up behind a driver who was putting gas into his empty tank on the entrance ramp to northbound I-71.

I got out to direct traffic, and as I did, I noticed a wallet on the ground. A glance at the driver's license and picture told me that the woman who'd lost it lived in Silverton, a few miles away.

Over the next several hours, I was absorbed by routine calls and forgot about the wallet, which I had laid on the front seat of the car.

Driving through a shopping center parking lot, I noticed an occupied car in a handicapped parking space, with no handicapped placard. The driver, a woman, was leaning her head against the steering wheel. She appeared to be worried or upset. As she looked up, I made eye contact with her; she nervously started her car and proceeded to move to another space, and I went on my route around the shopping center.

Suddenly I remembered the wallet and looked again at the picture on the driver's license. It resembled the woman I had just seen parked illegally.

I drove back around, found where she had next parked, and called in her license plate for an identification check. It was her!

I walked up to her car, and the woman quickly began to explain that she was waiting for her son. I smiled and told her I had something of hers. She looked confused. I then showed her that I had her wallet.

She jumped from her car, yelling, "Praise Jesus, praise Jesus, praise Jesus!"

She excitedly explained that earlier, just as I had pulled up, she had been praying that her wallet would be found. Then she raised her head from the steering wheel and saw me.

This shopping center was approximately two miles from where I had found the wallet. I would love to claim that my keen instincts and sharp observation as a police officer were the reason for this . . . but I know this was a wink from God.

Jeff

We've all had that sinking feeling when we lose something. It's disconcerting. Imagine the questions that must have come fast and furious to that woman when she realized she didn't have her wallet. "Where did I leave it? Did it fall out of my purse? Did someone steal it?" Yet, whatever her panicked thoughts, she had exactly the right response: she paused, took a deep breath, and prayed. Prayer centers us and calms our nerves.

The Bible tells us:

> *Come to me, all you who are weary and*
> *burdened,*
> *and I will give you rest.*
>
> Matthew 11:28 NIV

So when you've lost something, ask God to help you find it. He will settle your anxious thoughts and give you peace.

> *. . . Keep him in perfect peace*
> *whose mind is stayed on you,*
> *because he trusts in you.*
>
> Isaiah 26:3 ESV

30

How Can I Relieve My Apprehension About the Future?

Do not fear, for I am with you;
Do not anxiously look about you,
for I am your God. I will strengthen you,
surely I will help you.

Isaiah 41:10 NASB

Our aversion to change has much to do with our apprehension about the unseen future.

Yet fear of the unknown becomes less of an issue for those who have learned to stay in touch with God through prayer and who acknowledge that God speaks *back* to us through godwinks.

I would imagine that one of the most anxious times in

anyone's life is when he or she is going off to war. Notwithstanding the rush of excitement and thirst for adventure when they first signed up for military service, most young men and women must experience a high degree of apprehension about what they are about to face.

These are times when God often speaks directly to us in a most pronounced way, as He did with Bob.

Family Secrets

For some unknown reason, my mother told me about the existence of a cousin I never knew I had just after I joined up to fight in the Korean War. Why did she wait until then? I have absolutely no idea.

It seems that my father's sister, Helen Manfredi, had married a man with the last name of Reed, and she had given birth to a baby boy she named Robert.

Shortly after giving birth, Helen came down with tuberculosis, prompting her husband to put her into a West Coast sanitarium and leaving their child in the care of him and his mother.

When Helen was pronounced cured and released from the hospital, she tried to rejoin her husband and son but was turned away. Her husband and mother-in-law refused to allow her back into the home, afraid she would give TB to young Robert. So Helen had no choice. She stayed on in California for five more months, working at menial jobs, making every effort to rejoin her husband and child.

Helen was alone, lonely, and broke. Finally, family members on her side paid for train fare back to her former home in New York. Upon arriving there, highly distraught from what she thought was a conspiracy against her by her husband and mother-in-law, Aunt Helen suffered a mental breakdown and, at her request, family members agreed to never again mention what she had gone through.

But twenty years later, my mother decided to break her silence.

The air force sent me to Camp Stoneman, in California, which was a huge military port of embarkation. The base had about twenty-five thousand men constantly moving through it, to destinations unknown. Each person was assigned to a ferry to take us to the troop ships lined up in San Francisco Bay. My group was loaded on the troop ship *Frederick Funston*, and I was told to find an empty bunk. Stacked four high, the bunks were chain-held mattresses, eight to a unit, many decks below the water line.

With men scattering in all directions, I finally found an open slot. Another airman was also looking for a bunk. "That one's empty," I told him, nodding at the one next to mine.

He seemed nice enough, but two days passed before I asked the guy's name.

"Robert Reed," he said.

This seemed an odd coincidence, and I inquired further: "What was your mother's maiden name?"

"That's a funny question," he replied, looking at me. "Helen Manfredi."

I couldn't believe it! Here, by some strange godwink, I was meeting and bunking next to a first cousin I hadn't even known existed until my mother spilled the beans just two months earlier.

Well, cousin Robert and I got to know each other and became great friends. But when we landed in Alaska, we were sent to different bases. We corresponded for about a year—using only our military addresses—then lost track of each other.

I tried to find him again on a number of occasions, but without success.

Recently, I was telling my new neighbor Laurene about the godwink of my meeting my long-lost cousin right there in a bunk next to mine on a crowded troop ship. "What are the chances of that?" I mused.

Being a whiz on the computer, she offered to help me find Robert, to see if we could reconnect after all these years. Unfortunately, we discovered that he had passed away, as had his wife.

I learned that Robert Reed went on to be a noted physician in Indiana, a pioneer in sports medicine, and the national president of the Association for Children and Adults with Learning Disabilities.

I was able to connect with Robert's four children, who had great interest in learning about their grandmother Helen and things they didn't know about their father. We now correspond regularly.

Aunt Helen's wishes for secrecy had been so well honored

that when I told another cousin of mine that Robert had died, she said she had never heard of him.

I fully believe it was by some divine plan that Robert and I met. Somehow, each time I decided not to write this letter, something compelled me to continue. Divine intervention? You decide!

Bob Manfredi

What a powerful message of reassurance from above, directly to each young man, Bob and Robert, reminding them—through a godwink of incalculable odds, being bunkmates among twenty-five thousand others—that they needn't worry about the uncertain times ahead, that each would indeed make it through.

Godwinks can help you through periods of apprehension too.

If you are worried about the well-being of someone close to you, or if you're unsure about your work, your health, or your income, God wants to give you some certainty to replace those disquieting thoughts in your mind. He wants you to know that, whatever your circumstances, you can count on Him. He is always there. He will hear every prayer. He loves you and wants you to be comforted.

So do not fear, for I am with you;
do not be dismayed, for am your God.

143

I will strengthen you and help you;
I will uphold you with my righteous right
    hand.

                              Isaiah 41:10 NIV

It is when you feel apprehensive that you especially need to open your eyes to the winks from God. You'll soon realize that godwinks are like signposts on a dark and lonely road. They don't tell you *which* direction you should go—that comes from your personal choices and inner compass—but they will continually reassure you along your journey. Godwinks are tangible reminders of God's presence, offering hope and replacing apprehension with a genuine feeling of confidence that we can trust Him to take care of us.

31

Can I Trust God to Look Out for Me?

Be alert and of sober mind.
Your enemy the devil prowls around
like a roaring lion looking for someone to devour.

1 Peter 5:8 NIV

How often do you feel like the guy at the circus who spins plates on the ends of sticks, all standing in a row? He starts a bunch of plates spinning, then runs up and down the line, keeping the spin going so they don't crash to the ground.

Life can get so filled up—with things to do, people to call, places to go—that it makes our heads spin.

That's when we have to be on the lookout for the enemy. As I've said before, Satan loves everything "dis"—*dis*turbance, *dis*ruption, *dis*combobulation. When he has you *dis-*

tracted, he will try to *dis*pose of you through *dis*orientation, *dis*order, and *dis*cord.

Thank God for God.

When you're not on the lookout for *dis*ruptions in your life, God is watching your back.

And, if you've gotten into the habit of fortifying your daily life with prayer, you'll find yourself better prepared for emergency.

Just look at what happened to three of my readers who did just that.

Just-in-Time Godwinks

Wink 1

One Saturday morning I was on my way to Bible study and, as I often do, I was praying while driving. This particular morning, I was asking God for his protection. As I approached the corner traffic light, the light turned red; I stopped the car but continued my prayer.

When the light turn green, I took my foot off the brake to press down on the accelerator, but to my surprise, I couldn't seem to find the gas pedal! I even looked down to see where it was. I'd never had to do that before.

After "finding" the gas pedal, I looked up just in time to see a man driving an old station wagon—and running the red light.

At the speed he was traveling, if I had proceeded through

the intersection when I intended to, I would have been seriously hurt or killed. Praise the Lord, I was neither. I believe God sent his angels to prevent me from finding that gas pedal.

James

Wink 2

I've been in that position many times! I drive a school bus, often pray for my precious cargo, and have been saved from disastrous circumstances. I always say, "God is my copilot."

Nancy

Wink 3

I got into my SUV to go down the mountain to choir rehearsal, and, as I usually do, said a little prayer.

I hadn't moved more than five feet in my driveway when I heard a *pop*. My front tire was flat, and the vehicle was resting on the rim.

I discovered that my front coil suspension spring had snapped and literally harpooned the tire. My mind went back to the trip I had taken down the mountain earlier that day, traveling in torrential rain, at about fifty miles per hour. Thank God the spring snapped in my driveway and not while I was driving. With that godwink, I believe I was spared a nightmare.

Karen

Each of these readers were, thankfully, saved from the designs of the enemy and spared *dis*figurement or *dis*ability.

Like the writer of a well-known country-and-western song, they had asked, "Jesus, Take the Wheel." When James, Nancy, and Karen prayed for protection behind the wheel, God placed himself in the driver's seat and erected an invisible force around each of them, like heavenly Bubble Wrap.

Pray to him, and he will hear you.
Job 22:27 NLT

32

How Do We Know God Loves Us?

*Which of you, if your son asks for bread, will give him a
    stone? . . .*
If you . . . know how to give good gifts to your children,
how much more will your father in heaven
give good gifts to those who ask him!

Matthew 7:9, 11 NIV

God loves you.

"But how do I know?" you may ask.

We come to an acceptance of truths in our lives through
evidence. Our judgments, whether in a court of law or when
watching the news on television, result from an examination
of the body of evidence put before us, pro and con. Depend-
ing on our trust in the source, we come to a conclusion.

If we accept that the universe began with a big bang—a phenomenal explosion—fourteen billion years ago, it is because scientists say that's what happened and provide us with convincing arguments.

It just so happens that those arguments parallel what we are told in the Bible:

> *Then God said, "Let there be light,"*
> *and there was light.*
>
> Genesis 1:3 NLT

Based on that evidence and our trust in those sources, we can, ourselves, come to a reasoned judgment.

One of the best ways to accept the truth that God loves you is to see yourself as one of His children and to simply look around you at the massive evidence that exists. One source of evidence is this letter from a father named Shane:

Winks for Ayden's Army

My son Ayden and I were sitting in a store looking through books, and he picked up *When God Winks at You*—the one with the yellow cars on the cover—and said, "Daddy you need this book. I want to buy it for you."

I love the premise that many times in life, things happen that we pass off as coincidence when, in actuality, God is winking at us, saying, "Hey, at this moment, right now, I am thinking of you."

As I read the book, I could not help but think of times in Ayden's life when God winked at us.

In January 2010 Ayden was diagnosed with mitochondrial DNA (mtDNA) depletion syndrome. Doctors told my wife, Becky, and I that our son may not live to see his third birthday. To say that we were devastated would be a huge understatement.

In March we took Ayden to a dentist because of some staining on his front teeth. We found out that what was happening was far more serious than staining; his teeth were actually falling apart due to acidosis from the medicine he was taking to treat his disease. Ayden would need dental surgery to repair each and every tooth—the fourth time in six months he would be anesthetized, for yet another procedure taking several hours.

We felt upset as we left the dentist's office. Surgery poses a real risk for patients with mtDNA depletion: many suffer adverse effects after being put under.

On the way home, we stopped at a local store to do a little shopping. Like most two-year-olds, Ayden wants everything he sees. Luckily for us, if we let him hold the item while riding in the cart, he is content and will let us put it back on the shelves before we check out. The funny thing with Ayden is, he always insists we put it back exactly "where it belongs."

On that particular day, Ayden found a shopping cart and wanted to do some shopping on his own. As I followed Ayden up and down every aisle, he uncharacteristically was putting nothing in his cart.

At last we arrived at the greeting card section. Experience prepared me for Ayden's picking several that he "has to have."

Today, however, Ayden looked through the selection and picked up just one card.

He passed over those with Buzz and Woody and SpongeBob—even his favorite, Thomas the Tank Engine—selecting instead a religious card that would not seem particularly attractive to a two-year-old. He put it into his cart, and we proceeded to find Mommy.

On the way, the card fell out of his cart. I picked it up and read the simple message: "Behold, I will bring . . . health and healing" (from Jeremiah 33:6 ESV).

It struck me, at the moment, that it was a good sign; so I decided to buy it.

But here was the godwink.

Upon arriving home, we found an envelope in the mailbox from the Vatican. They wanted to let us know that someone had taken the time to ask for prayers for our child and that for the next sixty days, someone at the Vatican would be praying for Ayden.

Goose bumps covered my body, and my eyes filled with tears as I read the verse they had included: it was Jeremiah 33:6.

"Behold, I will bring . . . health and healing."

I could hardly muster the words to tell Becky what had happened.

I truly believe that God was speaking directly to us and was using two separate greeting cards to convey the message—a little wink.

Of the dozens of cards in the store, what are the odds of Ayden's picking up *that* one? We believe he was directed to it. It truly did help Becky and me to relax and know, down deep, that Ayden is going to be fine.

I now get the point: God sometimes sends us subtle little messages, and other times he has to hit us over the head to get our attention.

Thank you God, for giving us that godwink!

Shane Billingsley

Ayden sounds like a cute little character with a giant personality, doesn't he? It's obvious that he has the prayerful support of a loving family, including his earthly father, Shane. Meanwhile, our heavenly Father is looking out for Ayden—just as He is for you.

Every day, God showers you with an abundance of gifts. Yet it's easy to get busy, so focused on other things that you miss seeing them. A cheerfully chirping bird outside your window, heralding another breathtaking sunrise— that's a gift from God. The giggle of a newborn child and the exuberance of a playful puppy are gifts. Every amazing so-called coincidence that happens to you is an extraordinary gift—a person-to-person communication of reassurance—from above.

Only when you condition yourself to accept God's gifts and to thank Him for them accordingly, as Ayden's parents have, will you begin to see the massive evidence of God's love for you. By paying attention as godwinks unfold, you can begin to comprehend that they are special messages, specifically to you, out of seven billion people on the planet.

When Shane, Becky, and Ayden received a message, one out of thirty-one thousand verses in the Bible, from two unanticipated sources, the unbelievable odds helped them accept the evidence that this was a gift for them, a joyful message directly from God, saying, "Behold, I will bring . . . health and healing."

It was a confirmation that God cares for His children, including you.

> *See what kind of love the Father*
> *has given to us, that we*
> *should be called children of God.*
>
> 1 John 3:1 ESV

33

I'm Grieving Over the Loss of a Loved One

The wilderness and the solitary place
shall be glad for them; and the desert shall
rejoice, and blossom as the rose.

Isaiah 35:1 KJV

Grief comes in waves: first the pain, then the questions.

Losing someone who has been an important part of your life—here one day, then suddenly gone—brings pain unlike anything you've ever felt.

"Oh, God," you cry, "please make this pain go away."

Then the questions—rolling, relentless questions: How will I get by? Will I be able to take care of the finances? How will I get my own dinner, get myself to church, or . . .

or? Some of the questions make little sense. But, then, at a time like this, most things don't make sense.

The only thing that always makes sense is God, even when it seems that even He doesn't.

This is the time to speak with God in prayer and to listen for him to speak to you in his own unique way—a way that only God could—so you'll know that it is Him.

Here are two letters that may bring you some comfort in knowing that others have also sought to hear from God. The first comes from Justin.

December Roses—Toledo

My mom passed away suddenly last April at the age of sixty. It has been very difficult for my father, who is still living in their home in Toledo, Ohio. They would have celebrated their thirty-eighth wedding anniversary on December 7.

Roses always represented a symbolic connection for the two of them. My parents' backyard is landscaped with the many rose-bushes they planted and tended together. Every year since I can remember, Dad would buy Mom roses for their anniversary—as many roses as the years they were celebrating. Last year he bought her thirty-seven roses.

Roses do not bloom in Toledo in December.

Except for this year.

Just in time for their December 7 anniversary, my dad

looked out the kitchen window to see a lone rose, standing in full blossom, nestled in two inches of snow that had fallen during the night.

He went outside and stood there, staring at that rose, for about thirty minutes.

Was God winking at my dad with a heaven-sent message that everything was going to be all right? I think so.

Justin Keller

Can we even imagine how painful it must have been for Justin's dad to be without his dear wife on their wedding anniversary? Our hearts go out to him.

What a thoughtful man he was to give his wife the number of roses matching the years of their marriage. And what a sweet gift for God to give back, on a day when he knew Justin's father would be hurting most—a single, serenely blooming rose poking through the winter snow. It was a wink from God so special that it could not be mistaken.

In another letter—this one from Jonna—we can see how God again used roses as a means of special communication from above.

Yellow Roses of Tyler

My dear sweet mother went to be with the Lord just before she would have turned eighty-six years old. She was my best friend, and I miss her terribly.

Mom grew beautiful rosebushes at her home in Tyler, Texas, "Rose Capital of the World," and we displayed some of her spring roses at her funeral.

A short while later, my boyfriend, Garrett, and I were driving along a street we don't normally travel when he exclaimed, "Did you see those roses? Those are worth backing up for!"

Because there was no traffic, he put the car in reverse and began backing up so I could see those beautiful rosebushes. As the car began moving backward, we heard a disembodied voice coming from the backseat.

"That sounds like my mother!" I shouted, as we looked at each other in complete shock.

Garrett slammed on the brakes and put the car in park, and we both jumped out and started digging through bags in the back of the car. I then remembered that when my mother went into the hospice a few weeks before her death, I had purchased a digital voice recorder to record some of her stories. I had put the recorder in a side pocket of my briefcase in the backseat. Now, somehow, it had turned itself on and begun playing one of my mother's stories.

What is amazing is that to turn this recorder on or off, you must hold down the power button with a fingernail for four seconds; then there is a recessed Play button you must also use a fingernail to access.

I do not believe it was a coincidence that the instant we stopped to see the roses was the exact moment my mother's voice was heard. What a glorious godwink!

Jonna Fitzgerald

Here we have two different stories, from two different parts of the country, that have common denominators—the first being roses.

Did you know that roses are symbolic in the Bible and are mentioned many times?

Roses are one of the most perfect of all flowers. Perhaps that's why many Bible scholars believe it was Jesus who was being described in this Old Testament passage:

> *I am the rose of Sharon, and the*
> *lily of the valleys.*
>
> Song of Solomon 2:1 KJV

Another common thread in these two stories is the compassion God displayed for two people carrying the heavy burden of loss. It was as if God was whispering in the ear of Justin's dad, and to Jonna, saying, "Trust me. You will meet your loved ones again, and smell the sweet fragrance of the roses, in heaven."

> *For we know that when this earthly tent we*
> *   live in is taken*
> *down . . . we will have a house in heaven,*
> *   an eternal body made for*
> *us by God himself and not by human*
> *   hands.*
>
> 2 Corinthians 5:1 NLT

34

How Does God Use Doctors to Provide Comfort and Save Lives?

Give all your worries and cares to God,
for he cares about you.

1 Peter 5:7 NLT

Some doctors question the existence of God. Other doctors, who have witnessed seeming miracles and marveled at "coincidences" in medicine, have come to believe that God has cast them into divine dramas in which only He knows the ending; that through the grace of God, they have been provided with medical skills and tools that are in complete harmony with God's purpose for them to help people.

This leads me to wonder: Could God use doctors, sometimes without their even knowing it, to provide comfort and save lives?

You decide—here is Gloria's testimony.

Gloria's Fear

Before my breast surgery, I was scheduled to undergo a radiology procedure that was said to be invasive and painful. I was apprehensive and upset, and I prayed daily for comfort from God.

On the day of my procedure, I was teary-eyed and nervous. The doctor, noting my anxiety, tried to allay my fears by asking an odd question.

"How do you feel about first-graders?"

Thinking the question irrelevant, I told him that I love first-graders and that I had taught them most of my life.

"Yes, I know," he answered. "I was one of them."

Suddenly I looked up at him and saw the face of a child I had taught twenty-six years earlier. "Tommy Mannino, is it really you?"

He reached out, embraced me, and assured me that everything would be all right. And it was. I felt no pain. I felt only a loving presence that assured me that God was with me and had answered my call for help when I needed it.

Gloria

They will lay hands on the sick,
and they will recover.

Mark 16:18 NKJV

When we go through times of uncertainty, our human nature is to become anxious and fearful. The good news is that we have a lifeline that we can grab hold of at any time, day or night: the Word of God.

Don't allow the seeds of doubt and fear to enter your mind. You can't think negative and positive at the same time. So do what the Bible says:

Fix your thoughts on what is true,
and honorable, and right, and pure,
and lovely, and admirable.
Think about things that are excellent
and worthy of praise.

Philippians 4:8 NLT

Gloria received an extraordinary godwink just when she needed it. In the throes of a difficult medical situation, her desperate prayer was answered in a way she would never have imagined. What a pleasant surprise to discover that her doctor was one of her first-grade students from years before. How comforting to know that God sees every strand of our lives and knows just how to weave them all together.

When you allow Him, God will come into your life too—just when you need Him—providing godwinks of comfort.

> *He shall call upon me, and I will answer*
> *   him;*
> *I will be with him in trouble.*
>
> Psalm 91:15 KJV

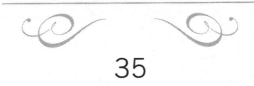

35

Where Am I Supposed to Go— What's My Destiny?

*Your word is a lamp to my feet
and a light for my path.*

Psalm 119:105 NIV

Sometimes you feel helplessly devoid of a rudder. Either you're going in circles or stuck. You wonder: "Do I have a destiny? Wasn't I supposed to hear about it by now? What is it?"

I've always liked this metaphor: You sometimes feel as though your life is a jigsaw puzzle dumped out on the dining room table. You paw through the pieces, exclaiming, "This mess is never going to fit together!"

But here's what you already know about jigsaw puzzles.

You believe that they will indeed fit together, if only you have the perseverance to keep at it, right?

How do you know that? You've seen the picture on the box.

So why can't you believe that the puzzle representing *you*—that jumble of pieces spread out on the dining table of life—will also fit together perfectly?

God has already seen the picture on the box of your life. He knows how all the pieces fit. So let's just get busy putting it together.

The situation this next reader wrote about might be similar to yours.

On-the-Job Winks

On a whim I picked up your book *When God Winks at You*. At the time I was finishing up months of training for a career my family was opposed to—mostly due to my age, and because I'm a mother with children.

I read the book here and there while going through a lengthy hiring process that included a lot more training and testing. I was getting weary of waiting to see what my potential employer expected me to do next, and I began to wonder if I had made the right career decision.

I dug into my duffel bag and pulled out your book. I opened it to the chapter on quests. I turned the page, and my heart skipped. It read: "Getting on Your Highway."

That was a major godwink that erased any concern I had about my career choice. You see, I was applying to be a professional truck driver!

At last, I got the job! So if you see an orange tanker out there, give a honk and say hello!

Liz

Just as God has a perfect plan for Liz's life, so He has a perfect plan for yours. All He needs is for you to "get on your highway," put your hands on the wheel, and say, "Where to, Father?"

When you do, He will give you everything you need to journey to your destiny.

What is your destiny? You never know for sure . . . not right away. But when you step out in faith and let God guide you, you'll begin to see the clues unfolding, one godwink after another. You may encounter someone unexpectedly— a Divine Alignment—and something that person tells you makes you think, "Ah, that's it—that's where I should be heading."

> *I will instruct you and teach you*
> *in the way you should go;*
> *I will counsel you and watch over you.*
> Psalm 32:8 NIV

As you apply God's Word to your life and remain in constant contact with Him, you will start sensing what

166

turns you should make and which direction you should be going.

Go ahead. Like Liz, get on your highway. Get into God's flow of traffic. Soon you'll be cruising smoothly to a destination that becomes clearer and clearer. You'll know it when you see it . . . it's your destiny.

36

What If I'm Lost on My Journey to Find Love and Happiness?

*All journeys have secret destinations
of which the traveler is unaware.*

Martin Buber

In my *When God Winks* books, I have urged you to conduct an archeological dig into your own life, to uncover godwinks that you may have dismissed or forgotten, for the purpose of helping you to understand that, all along, God has had you on His GPS: God's Positioning System.

"Go back to those times in your life when you came to a crossroads," I once wrote. "Make a list of 'coincidences' and answered prayers. This is what you'll discover: When there were multiple paths that you could have followed, there were always signposts of reassurance—godwinks of personal communication—directly to you, and no one else on earth."

Jerry Earl Johnston, a writer for the *Deseret News*, shared this delightful godwink story resulting from his own dig into the past—and what he uncovered about the time he fell in love.

Moses at the Drive-in Theater

Twenty years ago, when I was just getting to know Carol, I was on a trip and was pondering how I could convince her that I was just the guy for her. Spotting a postcard rack, I grabbed a card and sent it to her as a lighthearted hello.

The postcard was a random choice—a picture of a drive-in theater from the 1960s, jammed with cars, with Charlton Heston as Moses on the big screen.

I didn't know at the time how deeply the movie *The Ten Commandments* had affected her when she was younger. Nor did I know that the drive-in theater pictured was one she'd attended in northern Utah and the significance it held.

I just sent the thing.

But for Carol, it was like getting a calling card from the great beyond. I, the sender, was suddenly elevated to a lofty place in her mind reserved for a thoughtful, considerate person—one perhaps worth marrying.

That postcard changed everything.

I've wondered, "What if I'd sent her a postcard of four dogs playing poker?" Who knows whose wife she'd be today?

Jerry Earl Johnston

God helped guide Jerry in picking out the perfect postcard for Carol, which led to their finding a mate in life. But Jerry's story highlights another salient point. You need to act on those little nudges you get—his was to buy a postcard—because God can't help you unless you step out in faith and take action.

Perhaps you feel stuck; standing at a crossroads, uncertain which way to go. If you just stand there, waiting for your destiny to come to you, it may never happen.

Head out in the direction you believe to be the best, and godwinks will begin to reveal themselves like signposts in the fog, guiding you on the road ahead.

Surely sometimes, like the GPS in your vehicle, you'll need to recalculate—but a growing sense of certainty will develop that you are being guided by God.

How do you program God's Positioning System? By talking to the Navigator. He will never steer you wrong.

> *I will instruct you and teach you*
> *in the way you should go;*
> *I will counsel you and watch over you.*
>
> Psalm 32:8 NIV

37

How Can I Find Hope?

hope: |hōp| noun
A feeling of expectation and desire
for a certain thing to happen

Hope is a powerful force in life.

It's like going into the kitchen, turning on the faucet, and being surprised by the water pressure. You almost jump back, giddy that there's so much energy pouring out. Your hope is stored up inside and wants to burst out of you the same way. You need to turn on the faucet of your faith and then feel the surge of hope that springs forth.

If you are full of hope, you'll cause other people around you to almost splash, happily in your enthusiasm. Reinforced by the wonderful godwinks that happen to you, hope is contagious. Go ahead. Sprinkle it around!

My optimism and firm expectation that hope would spring up in every day of my life was due, in large part, to a hero I'd gotten to know: Dr. Norman Vincent Peale. He was a great preacher and the author of *The Power of Positive Thinking*.

I once heard Dr. Peale preach these words: "Hope! What a wonderful word it is! Write it indelibly on your mind. H-O-P-E. It is a bright word—shining and scintillating and dynamic, forward-looking, full of courage and optimism. With this word, let us begin each day!"[1]

You may be in such dire and difficult circumstances—such pain and heartache—that my suggesting that you should have hope is like insisting you can fly. It may seem like an impossible goal. Michelle thought so:

A Feeling of Hope

I have chronic pain from several facial surgeries and migraine headaches. I was feeling hopeless.

To look at me, you would never know that there is anything wrong. I'm forty-four years old, and I have a job, three beautiful children, and a new husband. But inside, I was feeling abandoned by God. Surely, if he loved me, he wouldn't put me through all this.

Not long ago, I went to visit some relatives. In the bathroom, on the counter, was a copy of *When God Winks at You*. It was opened to a page with a story about hope.[2] In a little box off to the side were the words I needed to see. It said (and I'm paraphrasing): Hope is the feeling that the feeling you are feeling isn't permanent.

Wow! I thought that was the best definition I had seen. I ended up reading the entire book.

That really was a godwink to me, because it gave me hope. The pain is the same, but maybe the future will be better!

Michelle

Perhaps you've felt like Michelle—carrying burdens that seem so very heavy; convinced that God has let you down. Maybe you feel that way now; life and circumstances have ganged up on you, putting you into a hopeless state of mind. You wonder, "How can I possibly find hope in this mess?"

> *May God, the source of hope,*
> *fill you with joy and peace through your*
> *faith in him.*
> *Then you will overflow with hope*
> *by the power of the Holy Spirit.*
> Romans 15:13 GNT

God is loving and merciful, even when he allows trials and sufferings to come into your life. The Bible tells us that God can be trusted to give you His strength to get through every struggle you face. He promises that you will have victory.

Helen Keller found victory. Her story was made famous by the classic film *The Miracle Worker*. Left blind and deaf by a childhood illness, Helen became a heroine for young girls as someone who could seize hope from hopelessness and convert it into a mission to help others by her example.

> *Although the world is full of suffering,*
> *it is full also of the overcoming of it.*[3]
> Helen Keller

In the final analysis, the answer to the question "How can I find hope?" is to turn to God.

> *Deep within you . . . nothing is hopeless.*
> *You are a child of God,*
> *and hope has been planted in you by God*[4]
> Norman Vincent Peale

38

What Difference Can I Make in Someone Else's Life?

We are therefore Christ's ambassadors,
as though God were making his appeal through us.
2 Corinthians 5:20 NIV

How many times have you thought, "Had I not crossed the street at that very moment, or walked into that place at that specific time, I wouldn't have met so-and-so, who led me to a whole new chapter in my life?"

I talk about this phenomenon as Divine Alignment, theorizing that there are invisible threads connecting us from person to person, event to event—godwink by godwink. I suggest that God helps to propel us toward the destiny He intends for us by making connections with others. Thus we can conclude that it was no accident that you met that "just right" person at "just the right" time.

Bill Bright, founder of Campus Crusade for Christ, told a story of Divine Alignment at ten thousand feet. I think you'll be inspired by it.

Godwinks in the Sky

When Pastor John Aker boarded a DC-10 at Newark Liberty International Airport, the plane was nearly empty. The computer, however, had assigned him a seat next to a man named Richard. Once airborne, the two began talking.

Richard had just come from the Sloan-Kettering Cancer Center. He had skin cancer. The doctors had given him ten months to live, at best. He was going home to Nebraska.

"May I tell you about something that changed my life?" asked Pastor John.

Richard nodded. John then explained the way of salvation and then asked, "Will you trust Jesus for your future? Would you like to know you are going to heaven?"

Richard clutched his hand and said yes.

Right there, at ten thousand feet over Chicago, John prayed with Richard as he gave his heart to Christ.

Months later, Pastor John again boarded a plane at Newark. This time he sat next to an elderly woman who was on her way to Beatrice, Nebraska. She told him her name. As they talked, John was amazed. It turned out that she was Richard's mother.

She told him that her son was still alive and growing in the Lord.

"I'm so encouraged," she said.

"Yes, and I'm inspired," said John, "that Richard has followed through and that God arranged for us to sit together."

The woman replied, "You know, this wasn't my seat. Just before you came on the plane, a woman asked me to change seats with her."

God does direct our steps. If we yield to him, he will use us. As we enter each new day, let's trust God to "arrange the seating" in our lives.

Bill Bright

How wonderful that God placed John Aker next to Richard. They surely will meet again in heaven.

Like Pastor John, we should all become ambassadors for Christ everywhere we go—even in the sky. In the Bible, Jesus invites us to share the good news of salvation throughout the world.

> *Go and make disciples of all nations,*
> *baptizing them in the name of the Father*
> *and of the Son and of the Holy Spirit,*
> *and teaching them to obey everything I have*
> *commanded you. And surely I am with you*
> *   always,*
> *to the very end of the age.*
> Matthew 28:19–20 NIV

If you have not yet become an ambassador for Christ, leading others to the Lord, you have missed a thrilling experience. When they accept Jesus, confirming that they wish for God to take them to heaven when it's time to leave this earth, their joy becomes your joy.

Watch for the people with whom God divinely aligns you—people you're seated next to on a plane or whom you encounter along your way. He may be providing you with the opportunity to be an ambassador for Christ.

39

I Feel Stressed About Health Issues

Do not be over-anxious, therefore, about to-morrow,
for to-morrow will bring its own cares.
Enough for each day are its own troubles.

Matthew 6:34 WNT

If you have a health problem, you likely are feeling some anxiety. Maybe a little. Maybe a lot.

Receiving a medical report that your body is functioning at less than optimum can be alarming. What can make it worse is when our minds start running away with us. We begin to "horriblize" all the things that *could* be. We worry about our survival and what will happen to our families.

In a letter from Vicki, it was easy to see how she and her whole family became instantly anxious about a medical report concerning her grandson, Jake. Yet, who could imagine that Jake was the one best prepared for the news.

Jake's Remarkable Book Report

Since first reading *When God Winks* and *When God Winks at You* several years ago, I have told everyone I know how life-changing they were for me, and I have given them to many of my friends as birthday presents. Yet I wasn't quite prepared for the godwink that happened to me in September.

It was a Saturday afternoon when my husband and I went to our son's house to watch a University of Texas football game and have dinner. Soon after we arrived, my nine-year-old grandson, Jake, said, "Mimi, would you please read my book report and see if it's okay? It's our first one for this year, and I have to turn it in on Monday."

I was thrilled to be asked, and we read it together, adding a few commas and correcting some spelling. I told him what a great job he had done, and he replied, "It really was an awesome book!"

It was. The name of the book was *Shoot for the Hoop*, by Matt Christopher, and it was about a little boy who loved to play basketball; but when he was diagnosed with juvenile diabetes, his parents wouldn't let him play anymore. Finally, the doctor and coach convinced the boy's mom that it would be safe, and he scored the winning basket.

That night, after the kids had gone to bed, I commented to my son and daughter-in-law, Amy, that Jake looked really thin. They agreed, and Amy said she had scheduled a doctor's appointment for Monday afternoon to have Jake checked.

I don't know why, but the odd thought that popped into my head was, "Jake turns in his book report on Monday morning."

On Monday afternoon I got an alarming call from my son, who choked back tears as he told me that Jake had been diagnosed with type 1 diabetes—also known as juvenile diabetes—and they were on their way to the hospital.

I was nearly speechless, struggling to process that diagnosis.

At the hospital, the doctor was amazed at the intelligent questions our young Jake asked, and we were all surprised that by the second day, he was giving himself insulin injections and doing the finger pricks to test his blood sugar by himself. People were awed that Jake seemed to know exactly what to do.

I knew immediately that it was a godwink. Of all the books in the library for him to have chosen for his book report, selecting that particular one—about a boy with juvenile diabetes—was not merely coincidence. I was sure of it. God had put that book in Jake's hands to prepare him for what was to come and to keep him from being afraid.

Many more godwinks associated with his diagnosis kept on coming. I am so grateful to you for enabling me to recognize them!

Vicki Chapman

Vicki reports that Jake is managing his juvenile diabetes like a trooper. And just like the boy in his book report, Jake is playing on the basketball team.

God has a divine plan for your life, and He will guide your every step. He knew all along that Jake would face medical issues, but He gave this young boy the ability—through godwinks—to handle his situation.

Jake's attitude can teach all of us how to react when we face adversity. He didn't allow his diabetes to be a stumbling block. He faced his trial head on.

God never said we wouldn't have trials and tribulations, but He does tell us that we can overcome them and even triumph over them.

> *Now thanks be unto God,*
> *who always causes us to triumph in Christ,*
> *and makes manifest the fragrance of*
> *his knowledge by us in every place.*
> 2 Corinthians 2:14 KJV

Jake was led by God to just the right book in the library for his report. When you face health-related stress, reach for God's book: the Bible. Some of your greatest peace will come from reading it. The Bible is God's personal love letter to you. Every bit of wisdom you will ever need is found in that one book.

> *It is the Lord who goes before you.*
> *He will be with you;*
> *he will not leave you or forsake you.*
> *Do not fear or be dismayed.*
>
> Deuteronomy 31:8 ESV

40

How Do I Deal with Disorder?

There is a time for everything
and a season for every activity under heaven
Ecclesiastes 3:1

When the 1960s musical group the Byrds sang their hit song "Turn! Turn! Turn! (to Everything There Is a Season)," perhaps only a few fans knew they were singing along with the Bible and God's plan for orderliness.

Writer Pete Seeger adapted the song entirely from the book of Ecclesiastes.

> *a time to be born and a time to die,*
> *a time to plant and a time to uproot,*
> *a time to kill and a time to heal,*

a time to tear down and a time to build,
a time to weep and a time to laugh,
a time to mourn and a time to dance,
a time to scatter stones and a time to gather
     them,
a time to embrace and a time to refrain,
a time to search and a time to give up,
a time to keep and a time to throw away,
a time to tear and a time to mend,
a time to be silent and a time to speak,
a time to love and a time to hate,
a time for war and a time for peace.

Ecclesiastes 3:2–8 NIV

Our God is an orderly God. He has a place for everything and puts everything in its place.

> *In the beginning God created the heavens*
> *and the earth.*

Genesis 1:1 NIV

By establishing that the earth will make one complete revolution once every twenty-four hours, He has given us time. The orbit of the moon around the earth marks a month; twelve turns equals a year. The result is an orderly cycle of seasons: winter, spring, summer, and fall.

The Byrds' song also brings to mind other wonders of God's orderly schedules: how our feathered friends know precisely when to fly north or south. The swallows return to Capistrano, California, just like clockwork, every March 19. And in the Northeast, where we live, the osprey can be counted on to return the first week of every April.

My point is, God loves orderliness.

I couldn't help but marvel at God's time and space engineering the day I wrote the following letter to Dr. Charles Stanley, pastor of Atlanta's First Baptist Church, whose weekly television program is seen in five hundred million households around the globe.

God's Perfect Order

It was truly a delight for Louise and me to visit with you in Atlanta for the first time.

I am compelled to share a remarkable godwink, which, as you'll recall, is the term I have adopted for those little coincidences that aren't really coincidence.

Your sermon, as usual, represented a magnificent teaching from the Scriptures. On Sunday morning you based your message on fifteen words from Psalm 37:4, "Delight yourself in the LORD and he will give you the desires of your heart."

The desires of *our* hearts were served just by getting to meet you. For so many years, as Louise and I watched your Sunday-morning broadcasts, I've concurred when she said, "I'd love to meet Dr. Stanley someday." Well, on Sunday, God granted that wish.

Yet we never imagined that when we briefly told you how we struggle to raise awareness for God on the island of Martha's Vineyard (our home, off the coast of Massachusetts)—and to explain that this location of a great revival in the mid-1800s is, today, spiritually starved—that we were also uttering the desires of our hearts, placed there by God, to help rekindle that flame.

That was confirmed when, not more than an hour later, you surprised us with a call to say, "I feel the Lord is telling me to come up there and preach."

Wow! We are thrilled that the outcome of those series of godwinks will be the Martha's Vineyard Inspiration Weekend this summer. We pray that in years to come, it will be evident that a spiritual revival was indeed the result.

But this is the godwink story I wanted to share with you: right after we received your call, Louise and I excitedly called our island preacher Jeff Winter to advise him of the good news."Imagine: our little church of fishermen and construction workers serving as the 'tug boat' helping to guide the huge vessel of InTouch Ministries into Martha's Vineyard harbor," I joked.

Before hanging up, we asked Pastor Jeff how his Sunday-morning services had gone in our absence.

"We had nice attendance," he said. Then he added, "My sermon was on Psalm 37:4, 'the desires of your heart.'"

Our eyes were wide with wonder.

The pastor of our ninety-member church on Martha's Vineyard had selected the same fifteen words from the Bible for his sermon that you, Dr. Stanley, had chosen to deliver on the same day and hour so many miles away in Atlanta.

I've since learned that there are nearly 800,000 words in the King James Bible.[1] The odds that two pastors who are on divinely aligned pathways to meet would preach on the exact same passage on the very same day are astronomically high.

Of course, we know that with God, there are no odds.

God gave us one more thing to ponder in his perfect design of things: I discovered that the geographic distance between Atlanta, Georgia, and Martha's Vineyard is 1,111 miles.

How perfect is *that* for Divine Alignment?

We look forward to seeing you, Dr. Stanley. We are convinced that God will fulfill the desires of each of our hearts: to find a new pathway to peace and joy through the Lord for many hurting, lost, and financially fragile people.

SQuire Rushnell (and the lovely Louise DuArt)

In the perfect world that God has created—with trillions of things working in harmonious order, from birds and flowers to space and seasons—isn't it reasonable to suppose that He also uses numbers—in this case Psalm 37:4 and 1,111 miles—to divinely align us with people and events so He can achieve perfect order for us?

We can also deduce that having a place for everything and everything in its place will help keep us aligned with His plan for us and our families.

*Be sure that everything is done properly
and in order.*

1 Corinthians 14:40 NLT

Establishing order is essential. Elizabeth Moermond, who works with a Midwest group called Simple Organizing Strategies, promotes the notion "that organization is fundamental to all other activities." She says, "When we place order in our own lives, we are giving glory to our awesome Creator God."

Elizabeth goes on to say, "Know that when you file papers, clean out and organize a garage, set up shelves in a basement . . . you are doing even more than bringing peace and order to yourself . . . you are praising and glorifying God . . . and at this, I think He smiles."[2]

41

I Wish I Could Take Back the Harsh Things I Said

Even if we feel guilty,
God is greater than our feelings,
and he knows everything.

1 John 3:20 NLT

I imagine this has happened to you.

You weren't looking for an argument.

Of course you were "in the right" . . . in the beginning . . . until you said all those hurtful things you didn't mean to say. They just sort of spilled out, as if from a closet crammed full of infractions that had been building up, stuffed in there for weeks and months. Before you knew it, the door to your mouth flew open, and every offense you'd been keeping to yourself came tumbling out.

Now you feel terrible.

That's the way Gerry felt. But his letter expresses how he discovered that God has an eraser for misspoken words.

Blue Winks

My sister was killed by a drunk driver in 1984, when I was fourteen. The night before she died, we'd had a terrible argument. She and I were constantly fighting—mostly because I had taken over the parental role as "Dad" in our dysfunctional family. Knowing that our last interaction before she died was so negative left me heartbroken and resentful.

My sister had grown more and more rebellious due to absent parents and their subsequent marriage split. Yet she was the only member of the family I talked to openly about my faith.

When she died, I wept uncontrollably and kept asking God why he had let this happen. More that anything, I needed to know that my sister was with him so I could have peace in my heart—not just about her but also in regard to the anger I had displayed just before her death.

My sister's favorite color was light blue. So I asked God to please give me a sign using her favorite color.

That night I was standing outside my favorite aunt's house when suddenly, up in the night sky, there appeared a beautiful, dancing, blue ribbon of color—the aurora borealis—which I had never seen before in my entire life. My aunt and I stared in amazement and wept at the sight of such a glorious sign from God.

Later, as we were preparing for my sister's funeral, a next-door neighbor came to our home. With tears streaming down her face, she handed my mother a beautiful, light blue dress and asked if we could use it for my sister. It felt like another sign from the Lord.

A day or so after the funeral, a friend and I were chatting, and she said, "Gerry, I've heard that if you receive a rose after someone's death, it means they're in heaven." Such superstitious beliefs don't sit well with me, so I just smiled and said, "That's interesting" and disregarded the idea. A few days later, I was cleaning out my sister's room and found a small New Testament that I had been given in fifth grade. Inside on a page in the back, I had recorded my personal commitment to the Lord by writing my name and the date. I flipped open that little book and saw, to my surprise and joy, that my sister had scratched out my name and written hers, with her own date of commitment in place of mine. I sat on the floor laughing and crying at the same time.

Within moments, my mother walked through the door and handed me a small vase with a silk rose in it. The rose was light blue. I was overwhelmed. She told me that this was all that remained from the funeral and, when she realized I had not taken any tokens of remembrance, she set it aside for me.

I kept that light blue rose for many years, and whenever

people would ask about it, I would tell them the story. God never ceases to amaze me . . . especially the way he speaks to his children.

Gerry Gionet

Gerry's story reminds me of when I was a kid and tried to understand the meaning of "forgive us our trespasses as we forgive those who trespass against us."

In the Lord's Prayer, we are given the pathway to making peace with ourselves for things we have said and done. Since God is willing to forgive us for trespassing against others, we should be willing to forgive those who have in some way acted against us.

God doesn't want you to live under guilt and condemnation.

> *God did not send his Son*
> *into the world to condemn the world,*
> *but to save the world through him.*
> John 3:17 NIV

If you are carrying guilt over something you've said or done and think it's too late to make amends, perhaps because the offended person has moved away or passed away, this is the good news: God still holds an eraser in his hand. Simply enter into a quiet conversation with Him, confess what you have done, and ask that He wipe you clean.

If any man be in Christ,
he is a new creature: old things are passed
  away;
behold, all things are become new.

2 Corinthians 5:17 KJV

God will wipe your slate clean.

As far as the east is from the west,
so far has he removed
our transgressions from us.

Psalm 103:12 NIV

42

How Do I Know That God Hears My Plea?

This is the confidence
we have in approaching God:
that if we ask anything according to his will,
he hears us.

1 John 5:14 NIV

Do you, on occasion, have days when you just have to lay your head on your arms and cry out to God for help?

You might have had the rude awakening of opening your checkbook and finding your funds depleted. Perhaps a doctor has delivered bad news. Or maybe you're at your wits' end trying to deal with someone or something that is stressing you out.

You wonder, "God, are you there? Are you witnessing this pain I'm going through?"

If you're truly open to it, you will receive a heaven-sent message—a godwink—an experience so delightfully unusual that you just know it had to come directly from God.

That's how Becky felt, according to this letter from Val.

To Becky: A Note of Hope

I didn't recognize the return address on the envelope as I pulled it from the mailbox. "Probably junk mail," I thought as I opened it.

To my surprise, there were two letters inside. Intrigued, I unfolded one of them.

"Dear Val," it began. That's me, but I had no idea who the letter was from.

"I hope you don't mind that I have located you. My name is Becky. Enclosed is a letter that requires an explanation. First, though, let me tell you a bit about myself.

"For the past several years, I have endured one struggle after another. The minute I get my head above water, something else pulls me under. Yesterday was one of those times. Going over some papers, I just put my head down and said, 'I cannot do this anymore.'

"This morning, I went grocery shopping, and in the parking lot I saw a folded sheet of paper on the ground next to my car. I thought it must be someone's grocery list, but something made me pick it up. It was the letter I have enclosed, written to someone with my name.

"'Dear Becky,' it read. 'You have been on my mind and heart a lot because I know you are hurting.'

"The letter contained a poem, 'I Am Waiting, Lord,' about having faith in difficult times. 'Lord, help me not to simply sit among my broken things,' one line read. 'Teach me in my waiting to find the valued remnants.'

"Even though I was not the Becky originally intended to receive this letter, I believe I was meant to see it. I do hope the other Becky got as much encouragement from it as I have."

Slowly, I unfolded the other letter. I did recognize the person who wrote this one. It was signed, "Val Ripka." Me.

I had sent that letter to my friend Becky when she was going through a rough time in her life. She had thanked me for my note when she received it—ten years ago. She said it had comforted her, but she later told me she had lost it.

Through God's grace, in spite of a decade in between, that letter was found by just the right Becky, at just the right time.

Valarie Ripka

Becky's note to Val brings to mind a passage from the Bible:

> *Your Father knows what you need*
> *before you ask him.*

Matthew 6:8 NIV

God knew Becky needed a boost of encouragement. And He knew it before she asked Him. He nudged her to pick up that letter in the parking lot, just to show that He cared.

Where had that note been for ten years, since its original owner lost it? Who knows? God does work in mysterious ways. All we know is the outcome. God employed Val to write a note, a decade before, that ended up lifting the spirits of two Beckys. That's a three-for-one-blessing, for in addition to boosting both Beckys, Val was blessed too.

Do you need a godwink today? Ask God for one.

A godwink may be one of those things you'd call a coincidence if you didn't believe it *must* have come from God. But a godwink is also an answered prayer. So go ahead . . . pray that God will wink at you.

Godwinks happen to you only when you allow them to happen—when you're willing to see and receive them. But once you see them, the more you'll see them.

The message of most godwinks is sweet: "Hey, kid . . . I'm thinking about you, right now. You're not alone."

Yes, Jesus loves me!
The Bible tells me so.[1]

PRAYER

43

How Can I Cope with Feelings of Isolation?

The LORD hears his people
when they call to him for help.
He rescues them from all their troubles.

Psalm 34:17 NLT

We can remember what it was like, as kids, to be shut out or shunned by schoolmates and siblings. When they locked us out of games or conversations, it felt hurtful.

In the history of some religious communities, shunning has been practiced as a form of punishment. A person would be locked out of all communication—disassociated from other members.

The feeling of exclusion and isolation becomes frustrating. They are in . . . you are out. It's similar to the feelings you have when you lock yourself out of your house or your car. You can walk all around the outside, but what you want is to be on the inside.

The emotional stress of being isolated came to mind when this letter arrived from Diane. She treats her being locked out with good humor, but you can imagine her feelings of stress before being allowed back in.

Locked Out? Call Calvary

One day I had to be at an interview by a certain time. En route to the interview, I noticed I needed gasoline. I pulled into the gas station, put gas in my auto, paid the attendant, and went back to my car.

The door was locked.

I didn't panic. I thought, "God answers prayers. Even little ones." So I prayed, "Lord, please send someone to help me."

As quickly as I prayed, a van showed up. It had a name on the side—Calvary Locksmith.

"Sir," I said, "could you please help me? I locked my keys in the car."

He said yes, and so thanks to Calvary, I made it to my interview on time.

And thanks to you, God, for winking at me!

Diane

Diane's delightfully lighthearted story underscores that when we're "locked out," God is the locksmith we can turn to. Instead of panicking, Diane prayed. And her answered prayer was a godwink. By sending a locksmith bearing the name we associate with Jesus at a time when He was isolated from everyone and hung on a cross to die, on Calvary, God showed Diane that He had empathy for her feelings of frustration at being locked out.

But let us turn the tables. Imagine how God must feel when we lock Him out.

Does He stand at the door to your heart, knock, and get no answer? Or do you immediately open the door and let Him in?

> *Look! I stand at the door and knock.*
> *If you hear my voice and open the door,*
> *I will come in . . .*
>
> Revelation 3:20 NLT

Is it possible that you have shunned God the way you were shunned on the playground as a youngster? Do you treat Him the way you are sometimes treated at the supermarket when the checkout attendants don't acknowledge that you're even there?

The King of kings is standing at your door. Go ahead. Open the door to your heart—wide—and invite Him right on in! The most important thing you will discover is how much He has loved you all along . . . even when you were ignoring Him.

How much does He love you? John tells us:

God so loved the world
that he gave his one and only Son,
that whoever believes in him
shall not perish but have eternal life.

John 3:16 NIV

That's a lot of love. Just for you.

The next time you feel excluded, the first door to open is the one to your heart. Invite God in. Everything will be better.

44

My Life Seems in Disarray

All things work together for good
to them that love God,
to them who are the called
according to his purpose.

Romans 8:28 KJ2000

If you've been to the musical theatre, this scene is familiar to you.

As you await the start of the performance, the curtain is drawn. You cannot see anything, but your intellect would tell you that behind that curtain, there is a whirlwind of activity. Sets are being placed on their marks; the actors are getting into position; the musicians are tuning their instruments.

Just before the stage manager cues the curtain to open, the

maestro picks up his baton and begins to conduct the orchestra. The notes, which sounded so sour moments earlier, during tuning, have now magically blended into a magnificent sound.

The curtain rises. The story begins.

In a way, your story unfolds like that too.

God is the great composer of your life. He orchestrates people, places, and things like a master conductor. You may not see it, but God is constantly working behind a veil of divine mystery. At any moment, perhaps when you are most in need of encouragement, He will raise the curtain on the surprise He's been preparing for you—a wonderful godwink to assure you that everything is going to turn out just fine.

Michael found that to be true, as he wrote in his letter.

Finding God on a Bike

My wife and I have been going through the most difficult year ever, with job losses for both of us. But things are looking up.

I'm returning to school with funding assistance from a government program, and my wife was anticipating a call-back for a job working with children in a before- and after-school program.

Yesterday my son and I took a long bike ride. On our return trip, we found ourselves on a bike path we'd never traveled before, and it came out at a school we'd never seen before. We became curious. It was a nice-looking school, but we couldn't find a name anywhere on the building.

Today my wife got a call confirming her hiring and informing her at which school she would be working. We looked it up
on the Internet, and to our surprise, it was the same school my
son and I had been led to the day before!

We've lived in this neighborhood for fourteen years; how we
remained unaware of a school that close—only five minutes from
home—is beyond us. But we did, and that's our godwink—proof of
God's handiwork all over our situation.

Michael McClure

Like Michael and his wife, you can be sure of this:
when the time is right, God will reveal His plan to you. He
is always active and working on your behalf.

Many times God chooses to work behind the scenes,
and we are unable to see or feel Him. If you are getting
discouraged, searching for evidence of God's presence, remember: He does some of his best work while you're waiting for the show to begin.

> . . . *I am going to do something in your days*
> *that you would not believe, even if you were*
> *told.*

Habakkuk 1:5

If you trust the Lord, you can be assured that nothing
will be out of place—nor one note out of tune—because
He is the Maestro.

45

How Can I Learn to Hear God Speaking to Me?

Now listen to me,
and let me give you a word of advice,
and may God be with you.

Exodus 18:19 NLT

We often hear people say, "God spoke to me."

What does that mean?

Most of us don't hear God's voice in an audible way. But when you actively engage in daily conversations with God, you place yourself into spiritual harmony with Him. And the more you participate in prayerful conversation, the more you'll feel that He's answering back—many times through what we call godwinks.

Other times you'll find that by opening up your heart and your spiritual eyes and ears, you will receive little nudges to step out in faith or to take action. It may be to speak with someone, to reach for a book, or to turn on the radio or TV to hear something God wants you to hear.

Marcia writes that she was surprised when God found a way to deliver a message of comfort to her at a time of great sorrow.

God's Ways with Winks

My son, my treasure from a prior marriage, bought me a *When God Winks* book for my birthday but forgot to give it to me.

Two months later, I was scheduled to travel to see my good friend Jim, a man to whom I'd frequently said, "You are the last person I think of when I lay my head on my pillow at night, and the first person I think of when I wake up."

However, with my suitcase half packed, I received the shocking news that Jim had just died.

I was devastated.

A few days later, knowing I was feeling down, my son and his girlfriend invited me over for dinner. They belatedly presented me with the book, and we read several stories to each other. I began to understand the meaning of godwinks.

A few days later, I was crying hard, still trying to understand it all, and I turned on the TV, hoping to find an inspiring sermon or something to comfort me. I happened upon a channel

I had never watched before—channel 45 out of Leesburg, Florida—
and an episode of *Little House on the Prairie* was playing.*

It was a scene where a girl was reading a letter she'd written to someone she'd recently lost. She said, "You are the last
person I think of when I lay my head on my pillow at night, and
the first person I think of when I wake up."

I sat there in astonishment. That was exactly what I used
to say to my dear friend Jim! And at that moment in time, I
knew God had heard me crying and sent me a godwink to show that
he cared.

So many times I've wondered: How could I, at that exact
moment in time, just happen to tune in to a channel I'd never
watched, exactly when it was playing a clip from a program with
years of reruns, and the actor's dialogue would be saying something no one else even knew I said to Jim, except God?

Does God wink? Yes. And if we pay attention, we'll know it.

Marcia Scott

What prompted Marcia to turn on the TV at that very
moment, to that particular channel? Might that have been
the Holy Spirit prodding her along?

When Marcia heard the exact words she used to say to
her dear friend Jim, she knew in an instant that God had
heard her cries—and that He loved her enough to send her
a special godwink to bring her peace.

Ask God to make you sensitive to the prompting of the

---

* Here's another godwink. The cable channel Marcia tuned in to that day was
GoodLife TV . . . and I was the network's president and CEO.

Holy Spirit too. If you feel it, go for it! The more you allow yourself to be led by the Holy Spirit, the more you will hear God's voice directing you.

> *For those who are led by the Spirit of God*
> *are the children of God.*
>
> Romans 8:14 NIV

46

How Can I Get Past My Lack of Confidence?

I can do all things
through him who strengthens me.

Philippians 4:13 ESV

It's hard to say how many times folks have shared with me the adage, "Coincidence is God's way of remaining anonymous."

At the outset, it seemed clever.

But then I thought it over.

No it isn't, I concluded . . . it's just the opposite. God never wants to remain anonymous!

One of the great teachings of the Bible is that God is

always available to you. If you're having a hard day or taking on a new challenge or find yourself on a pathway you've never traveled before—God is there! He's always available, and he's *never* anonymous. When you knock on His door, God is always home; and He always answers.

Consider Daniel's letter a confirmation.

The Sales-Rep Wink

After losing her job at age fifty-nine, my wife, Sally, was feeling rejected and uncertain about the future. She decided to join a well-known door-to-door sales organization that her father had been part of back in the 1950s. He had been so successful that he was awarded a gold, diamond-studded pin.

Sally had found the pin when her father died, and though she had no idea what it represented, she decided to wear it her first week on the new job—just a little something to help calm the jitters.

She approached a house in an upper-middle-class neighborhood, and an older gentleman answered the door. He politely listened to her introduction and then invited her in. After a short chat, the man stood up and said, "Let me show you something." He opened a closet that contained the same product that she was trying to sell.

Then he led her to two other closets containing more of the same products.

"Are you with this company?" Sally asked, somewhat bewildered.

"You might say that," he answered. "At least, I used to be." He explained that many years ago, he had been a company manager for this region of the state.

"In that case, I have something to show you," said my wife, pointing to the lapel pin. "This was awarded to my father in the fifties for his achievements with this company, and I am very proud of it."

"You should be," replied the man. "This pin represents an accomplishment not many people achieved."

There was a slight pause as my wife processed what was happening.

"Your father's name was Al, wasn't it?" asked the man.

Sally just about fainted. "Yes," she said. "But how could you know that?"

"Because I'm the one who pinned it on him!" the man said with a smile.

That day, Sally didn't "get the order"—the man surely didn't need more of her product—but she got something better: a wonderful little godwink that fueled her enthusiasm, long after, into what has become a successful career.

Daniel Livingston[1]

Of all the doors Sally could have knocked on that day, she was led to the home of the one man who knew the special meaning of that pin and could boost her self-esteem.

We all need encouragement.

When Sally placed that pin on her lapel as she went off to work that day, she was knocking on God's door. He did not remain anonymous but invited her in and greeted her with a wonderfully uplifting wink.

God is available for you just as He was for Sally. Come to Him, and tell Him that you, too, would like to receive messages of encouragement today—your own special godwinks. They will build your faith and give you hope.

> *Faith is the confidence*
> *that what we hope for will actually happen;*
> *it gives us assurance*
> *about things we cannot see.*
>
> Hebrews 11:1 NLT

47

How Can I Overcome My Feeling of Loneliness?

I will lift up my eyes to the mountains;
from where shall my help come?
                    Psalm 121:1 NASB

If you have suffered from loneliness, you sure don't need a dictionary to tell you what it feels like. But, in case you do . . .

Lone•li•ness (noun)
An unpleasant feeling in which a person feels
a strong sense of emptiness and solitude
resulting from inadequate levels of social relationships.[1]

Loneliness is something that nearly everyone is burdened with sooner or later. In fact, The University of Illinois reports that "one quarter of all adults experience painful loneliness at least every few weeks, and the incidence among adolescents and college students is even higher."[2]

I'm reminded of a song by Mariah Carey that reaches out to us: "If you're lonely and need a friend . . . keep the faith, and love will be there to light the way."

As believers we know that love and light are synonymous with Jesus. Look how He heard Betty's prayers and helped her through a difficult time of loneliness.

When You Are Feeling Low

I met a woman while I was out alone in a park and feeling low. I told her I was a widow. She said she was also a widow. Further, she said she had prayed to find a new friend to share things with, and she felt that she'd heard a voice telling her to go to the picnic table where I was sitting.

Since losing my fiancé to cancer, I, too, had prayed for a friend.

We went out to the parking lot and found that we'd parked our cars right next to each other.

We then learned that our birthdays are one day apart: September 8 and September 9.

I am so thankful that God showed his love with this godwink—my new friendship.

Betty

God divinely brought together two women with similar situations so they could help each other through a difficult time.

You may be feeling an emptiness similar to what they felt. Ask God to divinely connect you with someone who can understand your heartache.

> *Be completely humble and gentle;*
> *be patient,*
> *bearing with one another in love.*
>
> Ephesians 4:2 NIV

As Betty and her new friend walked though the valley of loneliness together, they realized that they didn't have to take residence there because God was taking them by the hand and leading them to the other side.

You can do the same.

Jesus is your best friend. He will never leave you or forsake you. He will be with you always—today, tomorrow, and forever. That's the promise of this old song:

What a Friend We Have in Jesus
Can we find a friend so faithful
who will all our sorrows share?
Jesus knows our every weakness;
take it to the Lord in prayer.[3]

ENCOURAGEMENT

48

Is the World Coming to an End?

Darkness cannot drive out darkness: only light can do that. Hate cannot drive out hate: only love can do that.
Martin Luther King Jr.

The headlines are frightening.

Terrorists plot to kill innocent people based upon lies fostered by fanatics, while disturbed children massacre schoolmates. Ravages of nature—horrendous tsunamis, earthquakes, tornados, and hurricanes—rip across the globe, leaving massive trails of destruction. We wonder if the earth and its people will ever live together in a peaceful state of harmony.

On the day of the Oklahoma City bombing, as we witnessed devastating death and destruction at the hands of a

217

single deranged man, one might have wondered, "Where is God in all this?" Rene had that question answered, and she writes about it in her letter.

God Is Still in Control Here

Many people don't know that I was at the Oklahoma City bombing in 1995. I was in college and working for First United Methodist Church next door.

I was running late for work that morning. I was supposed to be there at nine o'clock, but I had to stop by my mom's office, which put me behind. It actually saved my life. Had I not stopped by her office, I would have been right in front of that building when it exploded.

I arrived just minutes after it happened, and it was the most surreal thing I've ever experienced in my life.

I remember standing there looking at that building, the whole face of it blown off, with computers dangling from the fourth floor and paper floating down like snow. Stunned people walked around covered in gray ash and blood. It was utter chaos and devastation right before my eyes. But then I noticed something truly extraordinary.

At our church next door, which also suffered extensive damage, every window had been blown out . . . except for one. The stained-glass depiction of Jesus remained completely intact.

```
    I remember standing there, looking at that window in the
middle of all the chaos, and thinking, "God is still in control
here."
```

Rene Gutteridge

Even when things are turned upside down and inside out, God sees it all, and He is still in control.

> *God watches how people live;*
> *he sees everything they do.*
>
> Job 34:21 NLT

Yet He gives us free will, and some people choose to do evil things.

Our world is broken, and we live in dangerous times. Every day it seems to become more morally corrupt and spiritually starved. But we must not let our faith falter. God holds the future in His hands.

> *The LORD still rules from heaven.*
> *He watches everyone closely,*
> *examining every person on earth.*
>
> Psalm 11:4 NLT

Have faith. God is still in control here.

49

Can I Really Get in Touch with God Any Time of Day?

I call to God, and he will hear me.

Psalm 77:1 NCV

Can you imagine God standing on the moon, looking down at Earth?

We've all seen those photos of our planet looking like a big blue marble against the blackness of space.

But God can see right into the heart of every one of us scurrying around down here—all seven billion of us. I imagine Him musing, "My, my, they sure are busy."

God knows exactly where you are, day and night. He can read your thoughts. He watches your sins and applauds your good deeds.

Conversely, you can always reach Him. His office is open twenty-four hours a day. You'll never get a busy signal or a recording saying, "I'm not here right now." And you'll never get disconnected.

In fact, God is the God of connectedness. If *you* could stand on the moon and look through heaven-made night-vision-like binoculars, you might see invisible threads connecting all of us, from one person to the next, godwink by godwink . . . Divine Alignment.

I thought about that when this letter arrived from Steve.

Lost, but Found

I read this story in a Manchester, England, newspaper and thought it must be a godwink, so I wanted to send it to you.

Ken Whitty, sixty-four, who has been living in the small village of Reddish, Stockport, for the past decade, has been searching for his long-lost sister, Yvonne, much of his adult life. They were still kids when they were put into the care of a family friend after their parents died, and they lost touch with each other after moving away to start their own families.

"I tried to trace Yvonne many times," says Ken, "but to no avail."

Recently he decided to take one more stab at it by telling his story to the *Manchester Evening News*. Soon after his letter was published, he got a phone call: a woman's voice said, "Hello, this is Yvonne."

You may think that was the godwink. It wasn't. It's better.

You see, Yvonne is the woman Ken has been waving to from the street as he walked past her house for ten years. She lives just three hundred yards away.

"I just never recognized her," says Ken. "I couldn't believe it. I shot right round to see her!"[1]

Steve Woodburn

Sometimes miraculous godwinks are waiting for us right around the corner. But God waits for the perfect time to reveal them so we'll know the blessings are directly from Him.

Think of all those times Ken had tried to find his sister—for years—only to discover that he had already found her, just a short walk away!

God wants us to reach out to Him. He tells us that through the Scriptures:

> *In my distress I called to the LORD,*
> *and he answered me.*
>
> Jonah 2:2 NIV

Have you been wanting to get in touch with God? He is waiting for your call and wants to hear from you. As a matter of fact, before you even call, He's answering you.

Before they call, I will answer;
and while they are yet speaking, I will hear.
Isaiah 65:24 KJV

How do you dial him? Just clasp your hands, close your eyes, and speak to Him as you would speak to a friend or a dear grandparent. Pour your heart out. He knows what you're feeling and wants to help you carry your burden.

50

Is God Actively Involved in Getting Me to Help Others?

You alone are the Lord.
You made the skies and the heavens
and all the stars. You made the earth
and the seas and everything in them.

Nehemiah 9:6 NLT

From childhood we are mesmerized by God's magnificent design.

Do you recall marveling at the soft beauty of a daisy as you plucked its petals and let them float to the ground? Do you remember the jaw-dropping wonder as you looked at a night sky and said, "I wish I may, I wish I might, have the wish I wish tonight?" Or the sense that you were holding priceless treasure as a beautiful butterfly rested gently in your outstretched palms?

God's magnificent design is all around us. It is, therefore, not difficult to find His design in the unfolding of our everyday lives; how we "just happen" to encounter people and events to help us complete our tasks.

Jennifer is a designer of jewelry. Yet through this story, you'll see that she came to have a much greater appreciation for the Designer of all things.

Mystery Mary

My neighbor Brenda let me know her friend Mary McNamera was going through a rough time. Mary's husband had gone to the doctor for a lingering cold, been diagnosed with leukemia, and died within six weeks.

At the time, I was making jewelry—a hobby turned business. I created a bracelet with the crystal birthstones representing the birthdays of Mary's family members and gave it to Brenda to pass on to her.

Mary wrote me the most beautiful, handwritten thank-you note. I never actually met her, but I took notice of her handwriting.

Last January, Mary called. She reminded me who she was and told me she had met an amazing man, and they were getting married in July. She wanted me to add her new husband's birthstone to the bracelet. I was thrilled to make the changes for her and even happier that she had a new life and second chance at love.

I wrote a note, wrapped the bracelet, and added a *When God Winks* book to the bag, which I left hanging on the door for her to pick up. Mary later called, expressed her appreciation, and asked what she owed me. "Nothing," I said, requesting simply that she "gift it forward and do something nice for someone else."

Fast-forward to one year later.

My dad dropped my mom off at the door of the local Kroger and pulled away in search of a parking space. She tripped on the curb and fell. Her glasses broke, cutting into her eyebrow. Her arm was broken, mangled behind her.

A woman saw what happened, waved her arms to stop my dad, and rushed to my mom's aid. The woman called 911, sent her daughter for a blanket, wiped the blood from my mom's face, and was a kind, reassuring presence. She stayed with my parents until the ambulance arrived and, before it left, handed my dad a piece of paper with her name and phone number.

"Please call if I can help in any way," she said.

Mom underwent surgery to repair the broken bones in her arm. During her stay at the hospital, we heard much about the "angel," the woman in the parking lot who had been so helpful.

"Did you get her name?" I asked Mom.

"Yes," she said, reaching for the note with the woman's name and number. "It was Mary. Mary McNamera."

I was stunned into silence, then exclaimed, "Oh my!"

I called the number immediately.

"Mary," I said, "this is Jennifer. Do you remember when I asked you to 'gift it forward'? Well, you have no idea how you did just that. The woman you helped in the Kroger parking lot was my mom!"

In a surprised voice, she told me she'd just been praying for my mom!

We agreed to finally meet, over lunch, with Mom once she was better.

God winked!

Jennifer

It is part of Jennifer's personality to be charitable. Still, she had no idea that when she chose to do a nice deed for someone, God would return that kindness to her in such a personal way.

> *Let your light shine before others,*
> *so that they may see your good works*
> *and give glory to your Father who is in*
> *heaven.*

Matthew 5:16 ESV

We don't have to do something monumental to make a difference in someone's life. Small things count—sometimes as much or more than the bigger things. When you can "just be there" for someone, you are helping to complete God's design for your life—to fulfill your purpose. And you'll generally discover that when you extend yourself to others, your own problems seem smaller and more manageable.

> *Do not neglect to do good*
> *and to share what you have,*
> *for such sacrifices are pleasing to God.*
>
> Hebrews 13:16 ESV

When you help others, expect to see Divine Alignment unfold. As with godwinks, the more you acknowledge Divine Alignment in your life, the more it seems to occur. Every day, you'll "just happen" to encounter more people who play a role in getting you where you're going—even if just to cheer you along, reminding you of God's magnificent design for the world, and your place in it.

> *He will not forget how hard you have*
> *worked for him*
> *and how you have shown your love to him*
> *by caring for other believers,*
>
> Hebrews 6:10 NLT

51

How Can I Possibly Manage Impossible Tasks?

Be still, and know that I am God.

Psalm 46:10 NIV

Trying to figure out how to get through to someone; mustering the self-confidence to initiate the connection; determining how many follow-up calls you should make when that person hasn't gotten back to you; these are among the challenges you face every day.

And then there's the question: "What does *God* want me to do?"

Discerning God's will—versus your will—is always a struggle.

My wife and I have learned that when we arrive at such crossroads, we need to stop everything and listen. We seek a quiet place to pray, asking for God's direction; or we immerse ourselves in the wisdom of His Word; or, as an old friend once taught me, we write a letter to God.

When you do these things, the outcome will be amazing. During prayer, Scripture reading, or the act of writing to God, a fresh thought will pop into your mind—something that confirms the course you're taking or that opens up a whole new direction. As you roll this new thought around in your mind, you wonder if the idea came from you or from God.

Hoping He will identify himself, you sort through the pros and cons like you're adjusting a radio dial, trying to capture clarity from a distant signal. You're searching for the definitive voice of the Good Shepherd to lead you.

> *The sheep hear his voice,*
> *and he calls his own sheep by name*
> *and leads them out.*
>
> John 10:3 ESV

I admire producers, writers, and those who initiate movie and television projects. The seed of an idea is planted in an individual's mind and grows until it starts to blossom and needs to be shared with others—scores of others—directors, actors, producers, who begin to shape the idea, each according to his or her own perspective. Then there is the task of selling it to those who will see the idea from a financial perspective—whether it's a money-making or money-losing endeavor—the investors and distributors. The idea that once lived only in a single mind is adapted and challenged so many times that the originator wonders if it's still the same property. Compromise after compromise is made in the attempt to satisfy the demands and desires of each new player.

And all the while, one continues to ask, "What does *God* want me to do?"

This may describe the state of mind of Michael Frost Beckner as he wrote this letter. Michael's impressive string of scripts and movie credits notwithstanding, he had to re-establish himself with new people at every turn. Godwinks became signposts of sureness, telling him he was on the right path.

Let the Civil War Begin

I had been talking to my wife about my realization, as a teenager, that God sends us messages every day.

Finding your book about two hours later made me laugh out loud.

I'm a fan of your work in helping people recognize God, his attention to us, and his encouragement in our everyday moments. Here are two godwinks that have guided me in what has become the purpose of my professional life.

I am a successful film and television writer and producer. About nine years ago, I followed what I now realize was a call from Jesus to tell the true story of the American Civil War as an eight-hour dramatic miniseries for television; to reintroduce our nation to our greatest struggle and its meaning and lessons for our nation today, when it needs this story most.

When I presented the idea to my agency and manager or brought it up at network meetings, the response was universal: there was no interest in, and no market for, such a project. It was suggested that I would be crazy to spend time on such a noncommercial and "worthless" pursuit.

I decided to disregard these warnings and throw myself into the project. The research and major writing consumed me for the next seven years. Rewriting and fact-checking continues today.

The day I finished my first draft—more than eight hundred pages—I was leaving my office after saying a prayer of thanks to God for seeing me through the heavy-lifting part of this endeavor. As I pulled out of my parking space, I almost collided with a pickup truck.

I've worked at this location for over a decade, and this truck was not familiar as belonging to any tenant or customer of the local businesses. And I've never seen that truck again.

As the driver and I shared a wave—mine a bit embarrassed—as he drove away, I noticed his license plate: CVILWAR.

A frame around it read, at the top, "Grandson of a," and below, "Veteran"—the takeaway being that the driver was a grandson of a Civil War veteran.

Keeping in mind that I had just finished the first draft of my Civil War script, that was godwink number one.

As time went on, my detractors were proven wrong, and a talented, star cast came together to be in my production. I was headed to my first meeting with the actor who will play Ulysses S. Grant. At the time, he would have been the second attachment to the project. He was the star of his own successful television series, and I was nervous. I would be asking for his attachment based only upon good faith. I prayed that the meeting would go favorably, that he would see the value of this endeavor and volunteer to come on board.

My anxiety was soon assuaged as, once again, God winked. Driving on the freeway, heading for the meeting, a car pulled in front of mine. It was an out-of-state vehicle from South Carolina, and its vanity plate read: 4AM0412.

I think, to anyone else, that wouldn't even seem like a vanity plate. Only a Civil War enthusiast would know that 4:30 a.m., April 12, 1861, is the moment the first shots of the Civil War were fired by Confederate forces at Fort Sumter . . . in the state of South Carolina.

There is only one license plate, on one car from South Carolina, with that message. The odds of that specific car pulling in front of me—on a freeway 2,600 miles away in Los Angeles—as I'm on my way to meet the man who will star as the Civil War's greatest general are incalculable.

That is, without calculating in God's hand.

Michael Frost Beckner

What a charming letter showing us Michael's heart. Yet his journey is still long. Until his miniseries *To Appomattox* is unveiled for public viewing, he will need to stay in close contact with his Head of Production—God.

It is noteworthy that Michael's letter describes how he turned to prayer at each step of his quest and that the outcome was always the same: encouraging signs from above—amazing godwinks.

The odds that Michael would even see that reassuring message—on a South Carolina plate, miles from its home base, with a string of numbers and letters only a handful of people would be able to interpret—are truly astonishing. He instantly knew he was receiving a direct communication from God, providing support as he toiled on a large and complex undertaking.

> *The Lord directs the steps of the godly.*
> *He delights in every detail of their lives.*
>   Psalm 37:23 NLT

I can't wait to see Michael's miniseries, can you? Let's offer up a prayer for his success.

LOVE
TIMES OF SORROW

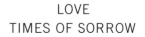

52

Can Love Really Last for a Lifetime?

Above all, clothe yourselves with love,
which binds us all together
in perfect harmony.

Colossians 3:14 NLT

How often do you hear of a couple, so much in love, that they resisted being separated long enough to go to the store?

On top of that, how often have you heard of a marriage that lasted seventy years?

Norma and Gordon Yeager were like that. Anyone in the little town of State Center, Iowa, could tell you that from the time Gordon proposed to Norma at her high school graduation, they were the "until death do we part" types.

And that's exactly what they became, according to this letter from their daughter Donna.

Inseparable Love

I want to share a story about my mother and father, who were very much in love, into their nineties, and who celebrated seventy-two years of marriage. Mother married Dad on the night she graduated from high school. But, it was how they *left* this world that captured worldwide attention in all the newspapers.

My brother Dennis and I always knew that our parents, Gordon and Norma Yeager, had a pretty unusual marriage. Other than a rare fishing trip, they were almost never apart. Didn't like being apart.

As they got up there in age, I began to worry what life would be like, if one survived, and the other didn't. I told Dennis, "I don't think they could get along without each other."

Meanwhile Dad, who was ninety four—three years older than Mom—would say, "I have to stick around. I can't go until she does; I have to stay here for her, and she'd do the same."

They went out for breakfast almost every day. One morning Dad pulled out at an intersection and apparently didn't see an oncoming car. There was a terrible accident. Mom and Dad were rushed to the hospital in the same ambulance, clinging to life.

It was touch and go for several hours. First we thought Dad

might survive, then Mom. And when nurses heard that Dad's blood pressure was falling rapidly, they rolled Mom's bed into his intensive care unit, placing the beds side by side. I looked over, and saw that they were holding hands. He was still hooked up to the heart monitor. She was not.

At 3:38 p.m., I choked back tears as I watched Dad slip away. Even when you think you are prepared, you're never ready for the loss of a parent.

As family stood at the end of their beds, we saw something strange. "Dad is no longer breathing . . . so why is his heart monitor still beeping?" we simultaneously asked the nurse.

She looked at us quizzically, then, pointed to Mom and Dad . . . still holding hands.

"Her heart is beating through him," she said, "It's being picked up on his heart monitor."

It was astonishing. Just astonishing!

Then, at 4:38 p.m., exactly one hour later, my dear mother caught up with Dad on the way to Heaven. The nurse said, "He's such a gentleman. He's standing there holding the door for her."

The crowning image for my brother and myself was seeing our two parents at the funeral. They were sharing the same casket. Holding hands.

I looked at Dennis and said, "You know, we were very blessed they went this way."

He nodded.

Thanks for letting me share this story with you. I hope it will bring blessings to any who read it.

Donna Yeager Sheets

In heaven, Norma and Gordon surely are celebrated, for they were one of those rare couples who lived their lives on earth divinely aligned, just as God intended.

> *A man shall . . . hold fast to his wife,*
> *and the two shall become one flesh.*
> Ephesians 5:31 ESV

When a couple takes their marriage vows seriously—to have and to hold from this day forward, for better, for worse, for richer, for poorer, in sickness and in health, to love and to cherish till death do us part—they are indeed worthy of honor.

> *Husbands, love your wives,*
> *Just as Christ loved the church*
> *and gave himself up for her.*
> Ephesians 5:25 NIV

In our ministry urging couples to take the 40 Day Prayer Challenge, we will long hold up Norma and Gordon as a model—a couple who lived their marriage as a trinity, three as one, themselves and God.

Thank You

We are grateful to the fifty-two or so people who took the time to share their inspiring stories of godwinks; an uplifting experience for each of us, wouldn't you agree?

We are also delighted that you have joined us on this spiritual journey. Perhaps you, just like those fifty-two, have encountered your own astonishing encouragements directly from God.

If their letters ignited a memory or two about the times in your own life when God winked at you, please feel free to share your stories with us.

As mentioned earlier, you can send your godwink story to any one of the following addresses:

- squire@whengodwinks.com
- facebook.com/GODwinks
- Godwink Stories
  P.O. Box 36
  Edgartown, MA 02539

We look forward to hearing from you.

SQuire Rushnell & Louise DuArt

Acknowledgments

A "leg up" is a term derivative of giving someone assistance. We all need a leg up once in a while.

Publisher Jonathan Merkh has consistently given us that kind of boost—first with *When God Winks at You,* then with *Divine Alignment.* Subsequently, it was Jonathan who inspired this little fun-to-write book, *Godwink Stories: A Devotional.*

Then, under the brilliant creativity and leadership of Becky Nesbitt, VP and editor in chief, and Amanda Demastus, associate editor, we have enjoyed a most exquisite relationship with our publisher.

Jennifer Gates and Todd Shuster, who give the term "literary agents" class, are fabulous "leg-up people" too.

Notes

Chapter 2

1. Civilla D. Martin and Charles H. Gabriel, "His Eye Is on the Sparrow," 1905.

Chapter 3

1. SQuire Rushnell, *When God Winks on New Beginnings* (Nashville: Thomas Nelson, 2009), 54.

Chapter 6

1. Luke 10:33–34, 36–37 NIV.

Chapter 8

1. "Divorce Rate," www.divorcerate.org, accessed April 16, 2012.

Chapter 10

1. "Laughter Facts," www.humor-laughter.com/laughter-facts.html, accessed April 16, 2012.
2. "Stress Relief from Laughter? Yes, No Joke," Mayo Clinic, www.mayoclinic.com/health/stress-relief/SR00034, accessed April 16, 2012.

Chapter 14

1. Adapted from "A Brownie for Brownie," Wink of the Week, April 24, 2010, When God Winks, www.whengodwinks.com/wow/wow_04242010.php.

2. www.hospicenet.org/html/talking.html, accessed May 6, 2012.

3. Candy Arrington, "How to Help Your Child Grieve," Focus on the Family, www.focusonthefamily.com/parenting/your_childs_emotions/how_to_help_your_child_grieve.aspx, accessed April 18, 2012.

Chapter 15

1. Adapted from "The Hug from Nowhere," Wink of the Week, December 9, 2010, When God Winks, www.whengodwinks.com/wow/wow_12092010.php.

Chapter 16

1. Adapted from "Don't Quit," Wink of the Week, January 15, 2011, When God Winks, www.whengodwinks.com/wow/wow_01152011.php.

Chapter 17

1. Bill Marshall, composer; ProudMusic.com.

Chapter 24

1. Victoria Rideout, *Parents, Children and Media: A Kaiser Family Foundation Survey*, the Henry J. Kaiser Family Foundation, June 2007.

Chapter 25

1. Jim Dailey, *Preparing for Eternity—On Purpose: A Conversation with Rick Warren, Decision* magazine, 11/1/04, http://www.billygraham.org/articlepage.asp?articleid=483; accessed 8/28/12.

Chapter 26

1. Jan Michael Joncas, composer; New Dawn Music; 1979.

Chapter 27

1. Carol Burnett, *One More Time* (New York: Random House, 1986), 263.

2. "Top Ten List: Grandmother Quotes," Sharp Business Solutions, www.inspirational-quotes-and-quotations.com/grandmother-quotes .html, accessed April 25, 2012.

Chapter 28

1. Recorded by Kathy Linden, 1959. Words and Music by Jack Vaughn.

Chapter 37

1. "Hope and Optimism," Inspiration for the Spirit, www.inspiration forthespirit.com/inspiration/food-for-thought/hope-and-optimism/, accessed April 27, 2012.

2. SQuire Rushnell, *When God Winks at You* (Nashville: Thomas Nelson, 2006), 82.

3. Helen Keller; Optimism; 1903; http://en.wikiquote.org/wiki/Helen_ Keller#Optimism_.281903.29, accessed May 7, 2012.

4. Norman Vincent Peale (sermon preached January 15, 1967) Vol. 18, no. 17 (Pawling, NY: Peale Center for Christian Living, 1967).

Chapter 40

1. http://agards-bible-timeline.com/q10_bible-facts.html;http://wiki.answers .com/Q/How_many_words_are_in_the_King_James_Version_of_the_ Bible; accessed May 8, 2012.

2. Elizabeth Moermond, The Spirituality of Order, a Christian Perspective on Organization, www.onlineorganizing.com/NewslettersArticle .asp?newsletter=ol&article=1092; accessed May 8, 2012.

Chapter 42

1. Anna Bartlett Warner, "Jesus Loves Me," Christian hymn, 1860.

Chapter 46

1. Name has been changed.

Chapter 47

1. Wikipedia, http://en.wikipedia.org/wiki/Loneliness; accessed May 8, 2012.

2. "Loneliness," Counseling Center at University of Illinois, www .counselingcenter.illinois.edu/?page_id=188, accessed April 30, 2012.

3. Hymnsite.com, #526, www.hymnsite.com/lyrics/umh526.sht; accessed May 8, 2012.

Chapter 49

1. Steve Woodburn retells a story written by Guy Patrick, www.thesun .co.uk/sol/homepage/news/article2090687.ece; accessed January 31, 2009.

GODWINK STORIES
CROSS REFERENCE

GODWINK STORIES CROSS REFERENCE